RIGHT-SIDE-UP IN AN UPSIDE-DOWN WORLD

KATHE S. RUMSEY
& ROBERTA M. WONG

WESTBOW
PRESS®
A DIVISION OF THOMAS NELSON
& ZONDERVAN

WestBow Press books may be ordered through booksellers or by contacting:

WestBow Press
A Division of Thomas Nelson & Zondervan
1663 Liberty Drive
Bloomington, IN 47403
www.westbowpress.com
1 (866) 928-1240

All Scripture quotations unless otherwise indicated
are from the King James Version

Scripture marked (NKJV) taken from the New King James Version®. Copyright
© 1982 by Thomas Nelson. Used by permission. All rights reserved.

ISBN: 978-1-9736-8767-2 (sc)
ISBN: 978-1-9736-8769-6 (hc)
ISBN: 978-1-9736-8768-9 (e)

Library of Congress Control Number: 2020904088

Print information available on the last page.

WestBow Press rev. date: 03/11/2020

Right-side-up
in an
Upside-down World

This belongs to: _____

Introduction

> Woe unto them that seek deep to hide their counsel
> from the LORD, and their works are in the dark, and
> they say, Who seeth us? and who knoweth us? Surely
> your turning of things upside down shall be esteemed
> as the potter's clay: for shall the work say of him that
> made it, He made me not? or shall the thing framed
> say of him that framed it, He had no understanding?
> —*Isaiah 29:15–16*

We live in challenging times and much of what has gone wrong in the world is the result of society taking God out of the public arena. Although hopelessness surfaces from every area of the world, God's people are never without hope. Over the past fifty years, the world has been turned completely upside-down. It is time to get quiet and hear personally from God, while building our faith.

Right-side-up in an Upside-down World utilizes a journal format to share biblical insights. The reader is encouraged to ask themselves if they are living by biblical principles, or by the world's standards and dictates. While the reader makes daily comparisons between what they hear in the news and what is taking place in their own life, they have the opportunity to record their observations and thoughts.

Believers must apply God's Word to their daily lives in these uncertain times. Christians can view the world's calamity with the peace of God that is beyond understanding. Hope for God's children results from their assurance that nothing takes Him by surprise. As believers prayerfully seek God's wisdom, and put it into practice, anxiety will not have place in their lives. Faith and hope will replace anxiety. God remains in control of everything contrary to what some may think.

Right-side-up in an Upside-down World represents a compilation of God's Word and personal insightful thoughts in a journal format for extended reflection. Some days the reader may have plenty of time to dig deeply into God's messages, and during those times it would be beneficial to use a King James Version of the Bible, a Hebrew-Greek Concordance, and a dictionary in order to dig even deeper into God's messages.

In order to live right-side-up, the reader must gain a deeper knowledge of God's Word through daily reflection of His truth that can be immediately put into action. This journal, as a long-term companion to one's Bible, will help the reader glean in stages wisdom and knowledge of the richness of Scripture.

In a world inundated with information and change, only the Bible contains God's wisdom that can offer mankind true hope for a better tomorrow.

This journal offers easily accessible pages to record important reference data for the reader such as: *Goals and Plans of Action, Dates to Remember, Blessings and Answered Prayers, Contacts,* and *Inspirational Resources.*

January ~ December

Dates to Remember

JAN:_____

FEB:_____

MAR:_____

APR:_____

MAY:_____

JUN:_____

JUL:_____

AUG:_____

SEPT:_____

OCT:_____

NOV:_____

DEC:_____

January - December

Blessings and Answered Prayer

_____

_____

_____

_____

_____

_____

_____

_____

_____

_____

_____

_____

_____

_____

_____

_____

_____

_____

_____

_____

_____

_____

_____

_____

_____

_____

_____

_____

January ~ December

Contacts

Name/Address/ _____
Home# _____ Cell# _____ Work# _____
Email: _____

Name/Address/ _____
Home# _____ Cell# _____ Work# _____
Email: _____

Name/Address/ _____
Home# _____ Cell# _____ Work# _____
Email: _____

Name/Address/ _____
Home# _____ Cell# _____ Work# _____
Email: _____

Name/Address/ _____
Home# _____ Cell# _____ Work# _____
Email: _____

Name/Address/ _____
Home# _____ Cell# _____ Work# _____
Email: _____

January ~ December

Inspirational Resources

BLOGS: _____

WEBSITES: _____

PODCASTS: _____

CHRISTIAN~RADIO: _____

CHRISTIAN~BOOKSTORES:_____

BOOKS: _____

The Messiah's Obedience

The Lord GOD has given Me the tongue of the learned, that I should know how to speak a word in season to him who is weary. He awakens Me morning by morning, He awakens My ear to hear as the learned. The Lord GOD has opened My ear; and I was not rebellious, nor did I turn away.

—Isaiah 50:4–5 (NKJV)

January 1
A new year is a brand-new start.

When assembled together with His followers, Jesus commanded them not to depart from the city, but to wait for the promise of the Father. When the Holy Spirit had come upon them, they received power to be His witnesses *(Acts 1:4–8; 2:1–4, 17)*.

Because the cares of this world constantly make demands upon our time and resources, how should we prioritize our daily lives? *(Mark 4:18–19)*. As God's children, we can seek Him for guidance and wisdom to know how to spend each day *(James 4:8)*.

> Let us therefore come boldly unto the throne of grace,
> that we may obtain mercy, and find grace to help in
> time of need.
> —*Hebrews 4:16*

Personal Reflections:

Without the Holy Spirit of God in my life, how will I have the power to be a witness for Christ? Explain how the gift of the Holy Spirit has made a difference in my walk with the Lord.

_____

_____

_____

_____

_____

_____

_____

_____

January 2

As God's children, we are to seek first the kingdom of God: His righteousness, His peace, and His joy in the Holy Spirit *(Romans 14:17)*. Love is the key to all of God's best. We must love as God loves—unconditionally.

> Little children, let no man deceive you: he that doeth righteousness is righteous, even as he is righteous. In this the children of God are manifest, and the children of the devil: whosoever doeth not righteousness is not of God, neither he that loveth not his brother. For this is the message that ye heard from the beginning, that we should love one another.
>
> *—1 John 3:7, 10–11*

Personal Reflections:

To avoid deception, how are the children of God distinguished from the children of the devil? If I do not unconditionally love others, how is it possible to be a child of God?

_____

_____

_____

_____

_____

_____

_____

_____

_____

January 3

Wake up! Live soberly. Live righteously. Live godly in this present age. Jesus will return for His bride when God the Father says it is time *(Matthew 24:36)*. The choices we make today determine our destiny. Are you ready? *(Revelation 19:7)*.

> For the grace of God that bringeth salvation hath appeared to all men, teaching us that, denying ungodliness and worldly lusts, we should live soberly, righteously, and godly, in this present world.
>
> —*Titus 2:11–12*

Personal Reflections:

What changes can I make in my life so that I live godly according to God's commandments in this present world? Which people, places, or things in my life hamper my ability to live godly?

_____

_____

_____

_____

_____

_____

_____

_____

_____

_____

_____

_____

January 4

God is specific in His Word how we are to conduct ourselves in the workplace. The circumstances we encounter are not to dictate how we behave. We are to respond with kindness and respect. To gossip about our boss or to do a poor job is displeasing to God *(Colossians 4:1).*

> Servants, obey in all things your masters according to the flesh; not with eyeservice, as menpleasers; but in singleness of heart, fearing God: and whatsoever ye do, do it heartily, as to the Lord, and not unto men
>
> *—Colossians 3:22–23*

Personal Reflections:

How can I in good conscience obey my boss when his requests are unscrupulous? Explain if it is okay with God for me to compromise my faith in order to protect my position.

_____

_____

_____

_____

_____

_____

_____

_____

_____

_____

_____

Kathe S. Rumsey & Roberta M. Wong

January 5

As Christians, we are to honor all those over us in our workplace, thereby redeeming the time. Instead of engaging in negative discussions about what is wrong, we must look for ways to make things better. It may mean going the extra mile to complete a project ahead of schedule, or assisting a coworker who is struggling to finish an assignment.

> Let as many servants as are under the yoke count their own masters worthy of all honor, that the name of God and his doctrine be not blasphemed. And they that have believing masters, let them not despise them, because they are brethren; but rather do them service, because they are faithful and beloved, partakers of the benefit. These things teach and exhort. Perverse disputings of men of corrupt minds, and destitute of the truth, supposing that gain is godliness: from such withdraw thyself.
> —*1 Timothy 6:1–2, 5*

Personal Reflections:

How might I make things better for my boss at work and for other employees? How can I genuinely love the person who is striving to take over my position?

_____

_____

_____

_____

_____

January 6

Today, the desire for prosperity has enticed and entangled many into foolish and harmful compromises. Greed and selfishness have driven them into self-destruction. Others have strayed from the faith because of the potential of easy wealth. As believers, we must flee idolatry, pursue our relationship with the living God, and allow the fruit of the Holy Spirit to reign in our hearts *(Galatians 5:22–23)*.

> But godliness with contentment is great gain. But they that will be rich fall into temptation and a snare, and into many foolish and hurtful lusts, which drown men in destruction and perdition. For the love of money is the root of all evil: which while some coveted after, they have erred from the faith, and pierced themselves through with many sorrows.
>
> *—1 Timothy 6:6, 9–10*

Personal Reflections:

How have I allowed the accumulation of wealth to take priority over my family and our life together? Why do I spend time at home doing work assignments rather than activities with family?

Kathe S. Rumsey & Roberta M. Wong

January 7

One vital tool that equips believers to overcome the challenges and obstacles of this world is to pray in the Spirit. The root of the problems we encounter from wrong behavior of others originates from the influence of spiritual forces *(Ephesians 6:12, 18)*. Have you received the baptism with the Holy Spirit? *(Mark 16:17; Act 2:4)*. Ask, and your heavenly Father will provide this glorious gift of victory *(Luke 11:13)*.

> Finally, my brethren, be strong in the Lord, and in the power of his might. Put on the whole armor of God, that ye may be able to stand against the wiles of the devil. For we wrestle not against flesh and blood, but against principalities, against powers, against the rulers of the darkness of this world, against spiritual wickedness in high places. Wherefore take unto you the whole armor of God, that ye may be able to withstand in the evil day, and having done all, to stand.
>
> *—Ephesians 6:10–13*

Personal Reflections:

How can I separate the undesirable actions of others from the dark spiritual influences that are driving them? How can I best utilize the whole armor of God for my protection?

_____

_____

_____

_____

_____

_____

January 8

As you renew your mind with the truth of God's Word, the transformed life you live will bring light and hope to others.

> I beseech you therefore, brethren, by the mercies of God, that ye present your bodies a living sacrifice, holy, acceptable unto God, which is your reasonable service. And be not conformed to this world: but be ye transformed by the renewing of your mind, that ye may prove what is that good, and acceptable, and perfect, will of God.
>
> *—Romans 12:1–2*

Personal Reflections:

How can I utilize my mind, will and emotions in service to God? What do I need to do differently if I truly desire to have the mind of Christ as I interact with others?

_____

_____

_____

_____

_____

_____

_____

_____

_____

_____

_____

January 9

In a perverted world that calls good evil and evil good, one must remain steadfast and cling to what is excellent. God's gentle nature within us makes a bold statement in the midst of selfishness and greed.

When faced with an individual who agitates you, ask God to reveal how He views the person. In cases where God is doing a redemptive work, His love will melt your heart and help you see others as He does.

> Let love be without hypocrisy. Abhor what is evil. Cling to what is good. Be kindly affectionate to one another with brotherly love, in honor giving preference to one another; not lagging in diligence, fervent in spirit, serving the Lord; rejoicing in hope, patient in tribulation, continuing steadfastly in prayer.
>
> Bless those who persecute you; bless and do not curse. Rejoice with those who rejoice, and weep with those who weep. Repay no one evil for evil.
>
> —*Romans 12:9–12, 14–15, 17 (NKJV)*

Personal Reflections:

How can I respond honestly and appropriately to someone who harasses me? Explain how I should respond to someone who does everything in their power to defeat me.

January 10

The financial world as we have known it is crumbling around us. Jesus commanded us to love others. Only relationships based upon God's unconditional love bring satisfaction in a world of excess and compromise.

> He that loveth silver shall not be satisfied with silver; nor he that loveth abundance with increase: this is also vanity. When goods increase, they are increased that eat them: and what good is there to the owners thereof, saving the beholding of them with their eyes?
>
> —*Ecclesiastes 5:10–11*

Personal Reflections:

How do I distinguish between a need, or greed? Describe what it means to invest my time in the true riches of God, or the deceptive riches of this world.

_____

_____

_____

_____

_____

_____

_____

_____

_____

_____

_____

_____

Kathe S. Rumsey & Roberta M. Wong

January 11

When we learn to be content and happy in whatever circumstance we find ourselves, then—and only then—will we be truly successful.

> I know both how to be abased, and I know how to abound: every where and in all things I am instructed both to be full and to be hungry, both to abound and to suffer need. I can do all things through Christ which strengtheneth me.
>
> *—Philippians 4:12–13*

Personal Reflections:

How can I avoid dependence upon the things of this temporal life to define my worth and happiness? What have I done lately for Christ that satisfied my eternal being?

_____

_____

_____

_____

_____

_____

_____

_____

_____

_____

_____

_____

January 12

As we deeply reflect upon God's Word and hear the voice of the Holy Spirit, do precisely as He directs. He truly wants what is best for us.

> For as the body without the spirit is dead, so faith without works is dead also.
>
> —*James 2:26*

> So then faith cometh by hearing, and hearing by the word [rhema] of God.
>
> —*Romans 10:17*

Personal Reflections:

Describe how I have prayed and personally heard a rhema word from God in the past. What do I expect when I lay hands on the sick and pray for a healing, or pray for a believer to receive a job?

_____

_____

_____

_____

_____

_____

_____

_____

_____

_____

_____

Kathe S. Rumsey & Roberta M. Wong

January 13

No longer is there time to debate the basic principles of Christianity. Everything we need to know is in God's Word. Seek His will and do not look back. Press on to maturity in Christ *(Ephesians 4:13–15)*. The wise must say—no—to the foolish and not squander their oil *(Matthew 25:8–9)*.

> Therefore leaving the principles of the doctrine of Christ, let us go on unto perfection; not laying again the foundation of repentance from dead works, and of faith toward God, of the doctrine of baptisms, and of laying on of hands, and of resurrection of the dead, and of eternal judgment.
>
> *—Hebrews 6:1–2*

Personal Reflections:

How do I pursue truth and receive maturity in my faith? What can I hope to learn as I read God's Word?

_____

_____

_____

_____

_____

_____

_____

_____

_____

_____

January 14

Flattery from a double heart can seduce and destroy a foolish person. In a world feverishly establishing its own moral code, conforming to the world's ideologies produces corruption. Immorality has seeped into every area of life. We must pray, draw near to God and resist the temptation to compromise *(James 4:8)*.

> They speak vanity every one with his neighbor: with
> flattering lips and with a double heart do they speak.
> The wicked walk on every side, when the vilest men
> are exalted.
>
> —*Psalm 12:2, 8*

Personal Reflections:

How would my neighbors describe me? What difference can I make in a rapidly deteriorating society, and what should I do when confronted by a wicked or vile person?

_____

_____

_____

_____

_____

_____

_____

_____

_____

_____

_____

Kathe S. Rumsey & Roberta M. Wong

January 15

The true victor in any confrontation is the one who is not moved by the words or actions of others.

> Wherefore, my beloved brethren, let every man be swift to hear, slow to speak, slow to wrath: for the wrath of man worketh not the righteousness of God.
>
> *—James 1:19–20*

Personal Reflections:

How do I respond to someone who has wronged me? What course of action do my emotions take when someone rejects my views?

_____

_____

_____

_____

_____

_____

_____

_____

_____

_____

_____

_____

_____

_____

_____

January 16

Jesus Christ is the Word of God, the Bread of life. He is the Bridegroom, returning for His bride without spot or wrinkle *(Ephesians 5:26–27; Revelation 19:7)*. When we study the Word of God, it keeps us focused and cleanses us as we wait patiently for His eminent return.

> Wherefore lay apart all filthiness and superfluity of naughtiness, and receive with meekness the engrafted word, which is able to save your souls.
>
> *—James 1:21*

Personal Reflections:

When I am tired, looking for something relaxing to occupy my time, do I turn to God's Word, or the television? What have I learned as the Holy Spirit leads me through truth?

_____

_____

_____

_____

_____

_____

_____

_____

_____

_____

_____

_____

Kathe S. Rumsey & Roberta M. Wong

January 17

In the Old Testament, even though God provided His commandments to His people, they wandered unsuccessfully in the wilderness.

In this hour in which lawlessness abounds, Christians must remain true to God's Word. His principles, which the world has cast aside, were not established to restrict our freedoms, but were intended for our protection. How much more are God's children wandering in the wilderness of the current culture! If we desire to live victoriously, we must obey God's principles outlined in His Word.

> But be ye doers of the word, and not hearers only,
> deceiving your own selves.
>
> —*James 1:22*

Personal Reflections:

When I read God's Word, how do I apply what I read to my own life? Explain how I view Scripture as the solution to my problems, and what results I have seen when I stand firm on God's Word.

_____

_____

_____

_____

_____

_____

_____

_____

_____

_____

January 18

The crown of life does not come easily in a world that is forever laying the feast of temptations before us *(Matthew 4:3)*. But temptation, like overindulgence, can be resisted and demands resistance if we desire to fulfill our Father's will.

> Blessed is the man that endureth temptation: for when he is tried, he shall receive the crown of life, which the Lord hath promised to them that love him.
>
> *—James 1:12*

Personal Reflections:

Describe how trials and temptations come, and how to handle them when they do. What does it mean to put God's love into action?

_____

_____

_____

_____

_____

_____

_____

_____

_____

_____

_____

_____

_____

Kathe S. Rumsey & Roberta M. Wong

January 19

Have you known someone who has no visible signs of wealth, but possesses inner riches that no one can take from them? Repent if you have judged anyone. Take the time to get to know those whom you may have misjudged in the past.

> For if there come unto your assembly a man with a gold ring, in goodly apparel, and there come in also a poor man in vile raiment; and ye have respect to him that weareth the gay clothing, and say unto him, Sit thou here in a good place; and say to the poor, Stand thou there, or sit here under my footstool: are ye not then partial in yourselves, and are become judges of evil thoughts?
>
> *—James 2:2–4*

Personal Reflections:

Have I caught myself being a respecter of persons? How can I become more like Christ Jesus and interact with people who are different than myself?

_____

_____

_____

_____

_____

_____

_____

_____

January 20

In our daily lives, opposition confronts us on every side, whether at home or at work. We will be unable to stand firm and give ourselves fully to the work of the Lord if we refuse to pardon the negative actions of others *(Ephesians 6:12)*. We must love others unconditionally and trust God to do the rest.

> Therefore, my beloved brethren, be ye steadfast, unmovable, always abounding in the work of the Lord, forasmuch as ye know that your labor is not in vain in the Lord.
>
> *—1 Corinthians 15:58*

Personal Reflections:

While seeking to fulfill God's plan for my life, what changes have I made? If I pray God's will only and not my will, what response might I expect from Him?

_____

_____

_____

_____

_____

_____

_____

_____

_____

_____

_____

January 21

When temptation comes, watch and pray. Use your time and energy to seek the truth of God's Word in all your circumstances. Worship Him only.

> It is written, Man shall not live by bread alone, but by every word [rhema] that proceedeth out of the mouth of God.
>
> —*Matthew 4:4*

Personal Reflections:

Have I experienced an opportunity to stand on a rhema word of God to sustain my life? What does a rhema word from God mean for a believer?

_____

_____

_____

_____

_____

_____

_____

_____

_____

_____

_____

_____

January 22

When we consider engaging in something we know is wrong, presumptuously thinking God will protect us because we are His children, we deceive ourselves. No matter what circumstances warrant, we must follow Jesus' example and speak God's Word when confronted with temptation.

> It is written again, Thou shalt not tempt the Lord thy God.
>
> —*Matthew 4:7*

Personal Reflections:

What does it mean to tempt God? What are the consequences of living for the world and not for God?

_____

_____

_____

_____

_____

_____

_____

_____

_____

_____

_____

_____

_____

_____

January 23

True repentance is the result of making a determined decision to turn from the behaviors of our past lifestyle that will draw us back into sin and bondage.

> And they that are Christ's have crucified the flesh with the affections and lusts.
>
> —*Galatians 5:24*

Personal Reflections:

As I walk with Christ, what must I do to keep my flesh from temptation? What can I do to turn away permanently from sinful desires?

_____

_____

_____

_____

_____

_____

_____

_____

_____

_____

_____

_____

_____

_____

January 24

To operate in the kingdom of heaven, we must humble ourselves as Christ humbled Himself in obedience to the Father. As we put off our old nature, the more like Christ we become *(Colossians 3:10).*

> Blessed are the poor in spirit: for theirs is the kingdom of heaven.
>
> *—Matthew 5:3*

Personal Reflections:

Describe how I have come to realize that without the gift of God's Holy Spirit in my life I can do nothing. What do I need to do in order to receive the baptism with the Holy Spirit?

_____

_____

_____

_____

_____

_____

_____

_____

_____

_____

_____

_____

_____

_____

_____

January 25

Our goal as God's children is to become partakers of His divine nature in all we do. Jesus prayed for His enemies; He did not retaliate evil for evil *(Luke 6:37; 23:34)*. What a privileged opportunity we have to become mature sons and daughters of God Almighty!

> Ye have heard that it hath been said, Thou shalt love thy neighbor, and hate thine enemy. But I say unto you, Love your enemies, bless them that curse you, do good to them that hate you, and pray for them which despitefully use you, and persecute you; that ye may be the children of your Father which is in heaven.
>
> *—Matthew 5:43–45*

Personal Reflections:

What is God's expectation of me as one of His children? How can I begin to demonstrate love to those who have become my enemies?

_____

_____

_____

_____

_____

_____

_____

_____

_____

January 26

There is no one except Jesus Christ who has offered complete redemption *(John 14:6)*. Time is short. Jesus is the One we must follow if we are to lead others into everlasting salvation. Share the truth as He leads.

> Follow me, and I will make you fishers of men.
> —*Matthew 4:19*

Personal Reflections:

Describe my willingness to be uncomfortable in the sea of life in order to go to where Jesus sends me. Explain a situation where Christ led me into uncharted waters as I followed Him.

_____

_____

_____

_____

_____

_____

_____

_____

_____

_____

_____

_____

_____

_____

Kathe S. Rumsey & Roberta M. Wong

January 27

To love the Lord our God with all our heart, soul, and mind means there can be nothing in our life that we love more. No one. Nothing. Scripture tells us that we cannot love God and have friendship with the world at the same time *(James 4:4)*. We make a choice daily. Love Him only.

> Jesus said unto him, Thou shalt love the Lord thy God with all thy heart, and with all thy soul, and with all thy mind. This is the first and great commandment.
>
> *—Matthew 22:37–38*

Personal Reflections:

If I am honest with myself, how do I love God with all my being? What changes do I need to make so that I can honestly call myself a Christian, a follower of Jesus Christ?

_____

_____

_____

_____

_____

_____

_____

_____

_____

_____

_____

January 28

Have you known times when you thought others needed to change, and then have the Holy Spirit reveal the changes you needed to make? We know from experience He gently shows us our error. A plank in our eye distorts our spiritual perception. If we adjust our eyesight to compensate our flesh, we only deceive ourselves. If we are to help others, we must humbly ask God to do a work in us first.

> And why do you look at the speck in your brother's eye, but do not perceive the plank in your own eye? Or how can you say to your brother, Brother, let me remove the speck that is in your eye, when you yourself do not see the plank that is in your own eye? Hypocrite! First remove the plank from your own eye, and then you will see clearly to remove the speck that is in your brother's eye.
>
> —*Luke 6:41–42 (NKJV)*

Personal Reflections:

Why do I judge others? What could I do in another's life to help them mature in their walk with God?

_____

_____

_____

_____

_____

_____

_____

Kathe S. Rumsey & Roberta M. Wong

January 29

Life can become a series of seeking after greener pastures. Throughout His life, Jesus submitted to His Father's will in all He said and did. If we are to accomplish God's will for our life, we must relinquish our individual desires and commit all our ways to Him. To achieve all the world has to offer and yet die without a personal relationship with Jesus Christ would be foolish *(Matthew 25:1–13)*.

> And he [Jesus] said to them all, If any man will come after me, let him deny himself, and take up his cross daily, and follow me. For whosoever will save his life shall lose it: but whosoever will lose his life for my sake, the same shall save it. For what is a man advantaged, if he gain the whole world, and lose himself, or be cast away?
>
> *—Luke 9:23–25*

Personal Reflections:

What am I holding onto in this world? If I knew something would keep me from spending eternity with God, would I continue to hold onto it regardless?

_____

_____

_____

_____

_____

_____

January 30

When was the last time you truly loved another person unconditionally? No matter what they said or did to you—you truly loved them. No matter what they added or took away from your life—you truly loved that person. For the world to know that we are followers of Jesus Christ, they must witness our unconditional love for one another.

> A new commandment I give unto you, That ye love
> one another; as I have loved you, that ye also love one
> another. By this shall all men know that ye are my
> disciples, if ye have love one to another.
>
> —*John 13:34–35*

Personal Reflections:

How do I demonstrate a genuine, unconditional love for others? Explain how my love for others is an active love that does not rely on whether they deserve to be loved.

_____

_____

_____

_____

_____

_____

_____

_____

_____

_____

Kathe S. Rumsey & Roberta M. Wong

January 31

Jesus crossed the barriers of time and space to die on the cross at Calvary in order for us to know God as Father. Mankind has no other way to God the Father except through God the Son, Jesus Christ. He is the only begotten Son of the Father *(John 1:14, 18; 3:16)*.

> Jesus saith unto him, I am the way, the truth, and the
> life: no man cometh unto the Father, but by me. If ye
> had known me, ye should have known my Father also:
> and from henceforth ye know him, and have seen him.
> —*John 14:6–7*

Personal Reflections:

Explain my confidence that my salvation is totally in the hands of Jesus Christ. What does it mean *to know Jesus is to know the Father*?

_____

_____

_____

_____

_____

_____

_____

_____

_____

_____

February 1

In a world that is building exponentially on quicksand, we can read and understand God's Word with the help of the Holy Spirit. He will comfort us and guide us through the maze of daily life. He is the Spirit of truth. But one day the Holy Spirit and the bride of Jesus Christ will be gone and the world will face the unrestrained, great tribulation.

> But the Comforter, which is the Holy Ghost, whom the Father will send in my name, he shall teach you all things, and bring all things to your remembrance, whatsoever I have said unto you. Peace I leave with you, my peace I give unto you; not as the world giveth, give I unto you. Let not your heart be troubled, neither let it be afraid.
>
> *—John 14:26–27*

Personal Reflections:

How have I found true peace? Describe how I seek fellowship with the Holy Spirit, and in what ways He has comforted, taught, and spoken with me.

_____
_____
_____
_____
_____
_____
_____
_____

Kathe S. Rumsey & Roberta M. Wong

February 2

True joy is not the fruit of our emotions or selfish ways. True joy comes when we keep the commandments of God and continue in His love. In a society that rejects God's commandments and wisdom is there any wonder why few people have found lasting inner joy?

> If ye keep my commandments, ye shall abide in my love; even as I have kept my Father's commandments, and abide in his love. These things have I spoken unto you, that my joy might remain in you, and that your joy might be full.
>
> *—John 15:10–11*

Personal Reflections:

How has the joy that was set before Jesus made it possible for me to endure my cross daily? What benefits have I experienced by keeping the Lord's commandments?

_____

_____

_____

_____

_____

_____

_____

_____

_____

_____

_____

February 3

As Christ's followers, Jesus forewarned that we would suffer the world's rejection and hostility; we will endure persecutions and experience hate's malicious sting. Nevertheless, it is better to experience the hate of the world than to participate in those things that God hates *(Luke 16:15; Hebrews 11:24–26; 1 John 2:15–17).*

> If the world hate you, ye know that it hated me before
> it hated you. If ye were of the world, the world would
> love his own: but because ye are not of the world, but
> I have chosen you out of the world, therefore the world
> hateth you.
>
> *—John 15:18–19*

Personal Reflections:

What does it mean to me to be accepted by the worldly crowd, the church crowd? Explain if it is possible as a follower of Christ to be loved by the world.

_____

_____

_____

_____

_____

_____

_____

_____

_____

_____

February 4

Persecution comes our way because we are not of the world. The Word of God instructs us to bless those who persecute us, bless and do not curse *(Romans 12:14)*. We have nothing to fear. Abide in God's love.

> Remember the word that I said unto you, The servant is not greater than his lord. If they have persecuted me, they will also persecute you; if they have kept my sayings, they will keep yours also.
>
> *—John 15:20*

Personal Reflections:

How do I react if others persecute me for my faith? What would I do differently than I already do?

_____

_____

_____

_____

_____

_____

_____

_____

_____

_____

_____

_____

_____

_____

February 5

Glory to God in the highest! As we gather in His name, Jesus is there. When Christians gather together to raise a family, do a project at work or reach out to help others, Jesus is with us. He is the only foundation upon which to stand when the things of this world attempt to overwhelm us. He is with us always and promised never to leave us nor forsake us *(Matthew 28:20; Hebrews 13:5).*

> Again I say unto you, That if two of you shall agree on
> earth as touching any thing that they shall ask, it shall
> be done for them of my Father which is in heaven. For
> where two or three are gathered together in my name,
> there am I in the midst of them.
>
> *—Matthew 18:19–20*

Personal Reflections:

What can I do to ensure my prayers are in agreement with another believer so our prayers will be answered? Where can I go to be in Jesus' presence?

_____

_____

_____

_____

_____

_____

_____

_____

_____

Kathe S. Rumsey & Roberta M. Wong

February 6

It is time for the children of God Almighty to grow up and to know who we are in Christ Jesus. Purchased with a price, we are not our own. God's love is so great that He sent His only begotten Son to die in our place so that we may share eternal life. If we truly comprehend these things, we will be innocent as newborn babes when it comes to evil.

> Brethren, be not children in understanding: howbeit in malice be ye children, but in understanding be men.
> —*1 Corinthians 14:20*

Personal Reflections:

When it comes to the things of God, am I settled or immature? Describe what it means to be apathetic to the dark wickedness that presently seduces many.

_____

_____

_____

_____

_____

_____

_____

_____

_____

_____

_____

_____

_____

February 7

To condone behavior that leads to death is neither being tolerant nor right; it is irresponsible. True love seeks a way to restore individuals to the path of life. Jesus never told people what they wanted to hear. He told them what they needed to hear. Pray, and then speak God's truth in love as the Holy Spirit leads *(Ephesians 4:15)*. It is God's will that none should perish. His children must walk in truth and love.

> Wherefore God also gave them up to uncleanness through the lusts of their own hearts, to dishonor their own bodies between themselves: who changed the truth of God into a lie, and worshiped and served the creature more than the Creator, who is blessed forever. Amen. For this cause God gave them up unto vile affections: for even their women did changed the natural use into that which is against nature: and likewise also the men.
>
> *—Romans 1:24–27*

Personal Reflections:

How should I respond to the social issues that contradict God's Word? How do I demonstrate genuine love toward others as God does, without ignoring sin?

_____

_____

_____

_____

_____

February 8

Today, seek God's wisdom concerning His will for your role in the body of Christ, then act upon what the Holy Spirit shows you. Do not deceive yourself, but be a doer of God's commandments, not a hearer only. We must obey Christ, the head of the church, in all things *(1 Corinthians 11:3; Colossians 1:17–18).*

> And he [Jesus] gave some, apostles; and some, prophets; and some, evangelists; and some, pastors and teachers; for the perfecting of the saints, for the work of the ministry, for the edifying of the body of Christ: till we all come in the unity of the faith, and of the knowledge of the Son of God, unto a perfect man, unto the measure of the stature of the fullness of Christ.
>
> *—Ephesians 4:11–13*

Personal Reflections:

In what way has Jesus called me to share His Word? How will I invest the time and effort required to truly study His Word and to share His truth?

_____

_____

_____

_____

_____

_____

_____

February 9

As we continue to grow in our relationship with Jesus and build our lives upon His doctrine, there remains no room for division among us. When we speak the truth and edify one another in love, we will walk in the unity of faith and the knowledge of the Son of God, Jesus Christ *(Ephesians 4:13, 15)*.

> Therefore leaving the principles of the doctrine of Christ, let us go on unto perfection [maturity]; not laying again the foundation of repentance from dead works, and of faith toward God, of the doctrine of baptisms, and of laying on of hands, and of resurrection of the dead, and of eternal judgment.
>
> *—Hebrews 6:1–2*

Personal Reflections:

How did I choose my church affiliation? How will I know God's reasoning for bringing me to a particular church?

_____

_____

_____

_____

_____

_____

_____

_____

_____

_____

Kathe S. Rumsey & Roberta M. Wong

February 10

God is pure. *Matthew 12:35* describes a pure heart, "A good man out of the good treasure of the heart bringeth forth good things: and an evil man out of the evil treasure bringeth forth evil things." Likewise, the words that we speak reveal the contents of our hearts. What we put into our hearts will come forth out of our hearts *(Proverbs 4:23; Luke 6:45)*. If the Word of God has taken root in us, then our speech reflects the work God has done in our hearts.

> But the LORD said unto Samuel, Look not on his countenance, or on the height of his stature: because I have refused him: for the LORD seeth not as man seeth; for man looketh on the outward appearance, but the LORD looketh on the heart.
>
> *—1 Samuel 16:7*

Personal Reflections:

How do I receive others into my life? How do I respond to the words of others, knowing that a person speaks out of the abundance of their heart?

_____

_____

_____

_____

_____

_____

_____

_____

February 11

Our present-day world is replete with strife and envy from one end of the globe to the other. However, as God's children, we are His house of prayer. Intercessory prayer provides opportunities for reconciliation regardless of our personal occupation. It is only through exercising His wisdom and authority that the world will come to experience God's peace which transcends all understanding *(Philippians 4:7; James 3:17–18)*.

> Blessed are the peacemakers: for they shall be called the children of God.
>
> *—Matthew 5:9*

Personal Reflections:

How can I become a peacemaker? Describe ways I can attempt to bring reconciliation among others.

_____

_____

_____

_____

_____

_____

_____

_____

_____

_____

_____

Kathe S. Rumsey & Roberta M. Wong

February 12

Our lifestyle of faith should create a desire in others to receive what we have in Jesus Christ. We must abide in the Word of God if others are to see a tangible testimony of the glory of God in our life. However, if we do not practice His righteousness, our life loses its savor; we will be ineffective witnesses for Jesus.

> Ye are the salt of the earth: but if the salt have lost his savor, wherewith shall it be salted? it is thenceforth good for nothing, but to be cast out, and to be trodden under foot of men.
>
> —*Matthew 5:13*

Personal Reflections:

In what ways do my actions preserve God's purpose for my life? Describe how I have allowed worldly concerns to drain the God-given vitality and creativity out of my life.

_____

_____

_____

_____

_____

_____

_____

_____

_____

_____

_____

February 13

One tiny light makes darkness flee. How much more would the unity of faith and the knowledge of the Son of God illuminate the world if Christians walked in His truth and love! Our actions and the words we speak should bring life and clarity to those around us. The united body of Christ collectively reflects God's love, mercy, and brings Him glory *(1 John 1:5)*.

> Let your light so shine before men, that they may see your good works, and glorify your Father which is in heaven.
>
> *—Matthew 5:16*

Personal Reflections:

How will others view God if my actions witness to His presence? Explain how I am motivated to glorify my Father in heaven by the things I do.

_____

_____

_____

_____

_____

_____

_____

_____

_____

_____

_____

Kathe S. Rumsey & Roberta M. Wong

February 14

This is the day in which the world will celebrate Valentine's Day. Historically, as Christianity spread, churchmen adopted a Christian meaning to this festival. However, this holiday originated from a pagan Roman festival called Lupercalia. Merchants would have us believe that flowers, chocolates, and exquisite dinners reflect true love *(1 John 5:21)*. As believers, we have received God's true, unconditional love. Daily, we are to extend His love to others.

> For God so loved the world, that he gave his only begotten Son, that whosoever believeth in him should not perish, but have everlasting life.
>
> *—John 3:16*

Personal Reflections:

How do I demonstrate the love God has for those who have failed to accept His precious gift of Jesus? How would I define sacrifice on behalf of others?

_____

_____

_____

_____

_____

_____

_____

_____

_____

February 15

God does not need our gifts. Have you ever received a gift from someone who gives it out of perceived obligation? It is not a blessing; you may even wish the person had not bothered. If we have division, strife, anger, or unforgiveness in our heart, and yet bring our gift to the Lord, He is not pleased. He commands us to love one another unconditionally as He loves us *(1 Peter 1:22)*.

> Therefore if thou bring thy gift to the altar, and there rememberest that thy brother hath ought against thee; leave there thy gift before the altar, and go thy way; first be reconciled to thy brother, and then come and offer thy gift.
>
> *—Matthew 5:23–24*

Personal Reflections:

In what manner was the love of Jesus demonstrated during his lifetime? When I have been wronged, how do I respond to the situation before coming before God in prayer?

_____

_____

_____

_____

_____

_____

_____

_____

_____

_____

Kathe S. Rumsey & Roberta M. Wong

February 16

God looks at our heart; outward appearances have no influence in His kingdom. His Word exhorts us to diligently guard our heart because out of the heart flow the issues of life *(Proverbs 4:23)*. Many times the difficulties and problems we face could have been avoided just by carefully guarding our heart. Without compromise, we must discern what we allow before our eyes.

> Ye have heard that it was said by them of old time, Thou shalt not commit adultery: but I [Jesus] say unto you, That whosoever looketh on a woman to lust after her hath committed adultery with her already in his heart.
> *—Matthew 5:27–28*

Personal Reflections:

What are my protective options when the seduction of sin bombards my life continually? How do I remove thoughts of compromise from my mind?

_____

_____

_____

_____

_____

_____

_____

_____

_____

February 17

We are day laborers in the kingdom of heaven. When asked by others or organizations to commit our time and talents, we must respond with an answer that is in accordance with God's will for our life. When we feel pressured or coerced to participate in an activity that we know does not align with His will for us, we must respond with —no—rather than make excuses. If we make excuses, we exhibit neither integrity nor character.

> But let your communication be, Yea, yea; Nay, nay: for whatsoever is more than these cometh of evil.
>
> —*Matthew 5:37*

Personal Reflections:

How do I respond when someone asks me to do something that does not fit my walk with Christ? Describe how I should respond in truth and love when asked to compromise my faith.

_____

_____

_____

_____

_____

_____

_____

_____

_____

_____

_____

February 18

At times, we find ourselves faced with invitations to company functions that we would prefer not to attend, but are obligated. Under God's direction, His children can view these requests as opportunities to bring Him as our guest.

Jesus did not turn down invitations to dine with tax collectors or sinners *(Luke 5:29–30)*. Sometimes He even invited Himself *(Luke 19:5)*. Jesus always brought truth and light into any assembly.

> And let us consider one another to provoke unto love and to good works: not forsaking the assembling of ourselves together, as the manner of some is; but exhorting one another: and so much the more, as ye see the day approaching.
>
> *—Hebrews 10:24–25*

Personal Reflections:

How can I take the initiative to meet with other believers on a regular basis? What are the signs of the Day of the Lord's appearing, and what should I be doing to redeem the time?

_____

_____

_____

_____

_____

_____

_____

_____

February 19

As a believer, what has God revealed to you to do in preparation for the salvation of your household? *(John 16:13; Acts 16:31)*. Do you have a prayer partner who diligently seeks God's face as you do? If not, it is time to find one *(Matthew 18:19)*.

Jesus demonstrated His love for us when He agreed to do what the Father asked of Him. Likewise, we demonstrate our love for one another through our obedience to whatever the Father asks of us *(John 15:12–17)*. True love requires sacrifice.

> By faith Noah, being warned of God of things not seen
> as yet, moved with fear, prepared an ark to the saving
> of his house; by the which he condemned the world,
> and became heir of the righteousness which is by faith.
>
> —*Hebrews 11:7*

Personal Reflections:

Like Noah, how do I train my ears to hear the warnings of God? What are my priorities when I know I have heard from God?

_____

_____

_____

_____

_____

_____

_____

_____

_____

_____

February 20

We need to examine our heart and ask ourselves if we truly live by faith in the Son of God. Are we willing to leave our comfort zone and follow Jesus Christ to receive our inheritance and promises? To live less would be foolish.

> By faith he [Abraham] sojourned in the land of promise, as in a strange country, dwelling in tabernacles with Isaac and Jacob, the heirs with him of the same promise: for he looked for a city which hath foundations, whose builder and maker is God.
>
> —*Hebrews 11: 9–10*

Personal Reflections:

How do I know I reside in the land where God chose for me? In what ways have I been faithful to occupy the community that God gave me by not allowing the enemy to take possession?

_____

_____

_____

_____

_____

_____

_____

_____

_____

_____

_____

February 21

God formed Jeremiah in his mother's womb. Before he was born, God sanctified him and ordained him to be a prophet. Likewise, God formed His only begotten Son, and each one of us in our mother's womb.

Throughout the world, abortions have claimed many innocent lives that will never fulfill God's purposes and desires. Truth may sting, but if we are salt, we must speak the truth in love and make a difference in this world. Jesus is the way, the truth and the life *(John 14:6)*.

> Before I formed thee in the belly I knew thee; and before
> thou camest forth out of the womb I sanctified thee, and
> I ordained thee a prophet unto the nations.
>
> —*Jeremiah 1:5*

Personal Reflections:

Have I stopped to consider in light of man-made decrees that God cherishes each and every baby in their mother's womb? How would I describe God's purpose for me in this world?

_____

_____

_____

_____

_____

_____

_____

_____

_____

February 22

If others offend us, it should be of no consequence. What matters is how we respond. How did Jesus respond to those who mistreated Him? How can we respond less? *(Matthew 10:24–25)*. If we do not love our enemies, how can we say we know God? *(Matthew 5:44–45)*.

> If thine enemy be hungry, give him bread to eat; and
> if he be thirsty, give him water to drink; for thou shalt
> heap coals of fire upon his head, and the LORD shall
> reward thee.
>
> *—Proverbs 25:21–22*

Personal Reflections:

Would I willingly give to my enemies if they had needs? Can I honestly say I would give out of my love and obedience to God and His Word, or grudgingly?

_____

_____

_____

_____

_____

_____

_____

_____

_____

_____

_____

February 23

Scripture tells us only half the expectant church will be ready upon Christ's return *(Matthew 25:1–2; 1 Thessalonians 4:16–17)*. Foolish choices will prevent us from being ready when Jesus Christ returns for His bride. How foolish it is to be engaged in reckless activities. We must redeem our time wisely. The Lamb's wife gets herself ready *(Revelation 19:7)*.

> As a dog returneth to his vomit, so a fool returneth to his folly.
>
> —*Proverbs 26:11*

Personal Reflections:

What types of things have kept me in bondage over my lifetime? Have I wasted money, eaten things that threaten my health, watched movies without value, or compromised my lifestyle?

_____

_____

_____

_____

_____

_____

_____

_____

_____

_____

_____

_____

February 24

As we put on the new man, we learn to control our emotions and our words. When situations arise that challenge us, we experience the pressure of temptations. If our own words condemn us, we need to change what we speak *(James 3:6)*. If we do not like what we hear from our own mouth, we can change.

> But now ye also put off all these; anger, wrath, malice, blasphemy, filthy communication out of your mouth. Lie not one to another, seeing that ye have put off the old man with his deeds.
> —*Colossians 3:8–9*

Personal Reflections:

When was the last time I allowed anger, wrath, malice, blasphemy, or filthy communication to come out of my mouth? How do I avoid conflict with others either at home or work?

_____

_____

_____

_____

_____

_____

_____

_____

_____

_____

February 25

Although removed from public display in our nation, the Ten Commandments cannot be removed from the hearts of men *(Jeremiah 31:33; Hebrews 10:16)*. God has delivered us out of sin's bondage through His Son Jesus Christ. We must pledge our allegiance to no other god. Anything or anyone that attempts to be first place in our life must be dethroned.

> I am the LORD thy God, which have brought thee out of the land of Egypt, out of the house of bondage. Thou shalt have no other gods before me.
>
> *—Exodus 20:2–3*

Personal Reflections:

How do I safeguard my walk with the Lord Jesus Christ? On what occasions have I been lured into the presence of other gods through exercise options, foods sacrificed to idols, or by false doctrine?

_____

_____

_____

_____

_____

_____

_____

_____

_____

_____

_____

Kathe S. Rumsey & Roberta M. Wong

February 26

God's first commandment clearly enumerates the things in heaven, things in the earth, and things in the water under the earth that are potential idols, even gods; things that can be worshiped or served instead of the Creator *(John 1:1–3; Colossians 1:15–17)*.

Trinkets and earthly possessions, as well as people, can become idols. We must not esteem anything or anyone above God. Worship God only. Future generations will pay the price for the iniquities of this generation of fathers. Some are already unknowingly paying the price for the iniquity their fathers, grandfathers, great-grandfathers and great-great grandfathers committed.

> Thou shalt not make unto thee any graven image, or any likeness of any thing that is in heaven above, or that is in the earth beneath, or that is in the water under the earth: thou shalt not bow down thyself to them, nor serve them: for I the LORD thy God am a jealous God, visiting the iniquity of the fathers upon the children unto the third and fourth generation of them that hate me.
>
> *—Exodus 20:4–5*

Personal Reflections:

What is my motive when I surround myself with things or shrines that represent a specific brand or image? Have I subjected my children to the seduction of trendy trinkets of the world?

February 27

If we call ourselves Christian, but live contrary to the truth of the gospel, are we taking God's name in vain? If we continue to walk in darkness, our spiritual lives will bear no fruit.

> This then is the message which we have heard of him, and declare unto you, that God is light, and in him is no darkness at all. If we say that we have fellowship with him, and walk in darkness, we lie, and do not the truth.
>
> —*1 John 1:5–6*

Personal Reflections:

Explain an experience where I have walked into a building and felt an eerie darkness. Will God send me into a bar to minister, or would He take me to another place to cross paths with someone?

_____

_____

_____

_____

_____

_____

_____

_____

_____

_____

_____

_____

Kathe S. Rumsey & Roberta M. Wong

February 28

In past generations, our nation honored Sunday as a day for God, family, and friends. Some may remember when stores began to remain open for business on Sundays. It was shocking at first, and most Christians would not participate.

As priorities changed, society changed. These negative consequences made a powerful impact upon family life. Idolatry and division followed. Brokenness has resulted. We are reminded in *Mark 2:27* that the sabbath was made for man, and not man for the sabbath.

> Remember the sabbath day to keep it holy. Six days shalt thou labor, and do all thy work: but the seventh day is the sabbath of the LORD thy God...For in six days the LORD made heaven and earth, the sea, and all that in them is, and rested the seventh day: wherefore the LORD blessed the sabbath day, and hallowed it.
>
> —*Exodus 20:8–11*

Personal Reflections:

What are some positive ways to rest and spend time with God on Sunday, or the Sabbath? How might I do chores at home throughout the week, so that I may spend time on Sunday with God?

_____

_____

_____

_____

_____

_____

March 1

The world considers you weak if you do not get even with others for everything they do to you. God tells us not only to take it once, but also to turn the other cheek. If we are to be right-side-up in an upside-down world, we must forgive others of their offenses against us *(James 2:8)*. Obedience to God and His Word is the bottom line in any situation.

> Ye have heard that it hath been said, An eye for an eye,
> and a tooth for a tooth: but I [Jesus] say unto you, That
> ye resist not evil: but whosoever shall smite thee on thy
> right cheek, turn to him the other also.
>
> —*Matthew 5:38–39*

Personal Reflections:

How do I feel when I obey God? How long have I trusted God's Word and the Holy Spirit to guide me, knowing His kingdom operates differently than the world's systems?

_____

_____

_____

_____

_____

_____

_____

_____

_____

_____

March 2

Jesus has provided us with a guide for prayer. The key to prayer is "after this manner," pray. He instructs us to direct our prayers to our heavenly Father. As our kinsman-redeemer, Jesus Christ established this new relationship for us. Believers can approach Almighty God, the Creator and Ruler of the universe, as His very own sons and daughters. God loves His children, and once we make known our requests to Him, He will always respond with our best interest at heart.

> After this manner therefore pray ye: Our Father which art in heaven.
>
> —*Matthew 6:9*

Personal Reflections:

Which way have I learned to pray: by memorization, from my heart directly to my heavenly Father, or in my prayer language (Ephesians 6:18)? What determines whether my prayers are answered?

_____

_____

_____

_____

_____

_____

_____

_____

_____

_____

March 3

If we had all the money in the world, it would still not satisfy the inner longings of the heart. This truth is evident today. Believers should never sacrifice the true riches of God for the sake of the supposed wealth the world offers.

Followers of Christ need to be more aware of what they say. If we speak about inappropriate movies, song lyrics or books just to avoid rejection, then we rob others and ourselves of God's best. When we elect to participate in these discussions, we prevent others from receiving something of greater value: the realization that a personal relationship with Jesus Christ is the greatest treasure of all.

> Lay not up for yourselves treasures upon the earth, where moth and rust doth corrupt, and where thieves break through and steal: but lay up for yourselves treasures in heaven, where neither moth nor rust doth corrupt, and where thieves do not break through nor steal: for where your treasure is, there will your heart be also.
>
> —*Matthew 6:19–21*

Personal Reflections:

When I look around my home, have I accumulated family mementos, or worldly idols? How would I recognize the true treasures of God if they were before me?

_____

_____

_____

_____

March 4

In an affluent world, there are more than enough possessions to meet everyone's needs. God's family does not suffer lack. He provides for our needs in ways we could never have imagined.

One of these days, Jesus will return for those who are watching for Him. It is time to let go of the things that keep us bound to this world *(Matthew 6:33)*.

> Give to him that asketh thee, and from him that would
> borrow of thee turn not thou away.
>
> *—Matthew 5:42*

Personal Reflections:

What is my response when someone requests something from me, yet I know it would not be good for them? How do I respond to a neighbor, or another person who habitually wants to borrow?

_____

_____

_____

_____

_____

_____

_____

_____

_____

_____

_____

_____

_____

March 5

Charitable organizations inundate us with their incessant requests for support. For all the generous outpouring to these institutions, we have yet to eradicate poverty and disease. Only God has the wisdom and insight we need to help us resolve the problems of mankind. We must seek Him for direction regarding our donations *(Colossians 2:2–3)*.

> Take heed that ye do not your alms [charitable deeds] before men, to be seen of them: otherwise ye have no reward of your Father which is in heaven.
>
> *—Matthew 6:1*

Personal Reflections:

Where do I seek approval in my life, is it from God or other people? What are my options when I am asked for charitable donations?

_____

_____

_____

_____

_____

_____

_____

_____

_____

_____

_____

Kathe S. Rumsey & Roberta M. Wong

March 6

Charities and corporate America have become big business partners. Everywhere pressure to give to this cause or that charity confronts us.

As God's children, instead of giving automatically through payroll deductions or instantly with our credit cards, we have alternatives. When we seek God's guidance, He will show us new ways to meet genuine need. What can we do to bless a widow, the elderly, or a child? What do we have in our homes that would meet someone else's need? Do we have a skill to share that would meet another's need? The Holy Spirit will lead us. The church must not follow the world and coerce others into giving *(2 Corinthians 9:6–7)*.

> But when thou doest alms [charitable deeds], let not thy left hand know what thy right hand doeth: that thine alms may be in secret: and thy Father which seeth in secret himself shall reward thee openly.
>
> *—Matthew 6:3–4*

Personal Reflections:

How proper is it for a Christian to declare their charitable giving publicly? What motivates me to give: it looks like a good cause, a friend's influence, or because the Holy Spirit leads me to give?

_____

_____

_____

_____

_____

_____

March 7

Prayer is a cherished opportunity to communicate with God. He has a divine plan for each one of us, to bless us and not to condemn us *(Jeremiah 29:11)*. We must seek Him early today with all our heart. Ask Him for wisdom and direction for the next twenty-four hours, and then follow His advice. The richness of a day well spent with God is our reward.

> But thou, when thou prayest, enter into thy closet, and
> when thou hast shut thy door, pray to thy Father which
> is in secret: and thy Father which seeth in secret shall
> reward thee openly.
> —*Matthew 6:6*

Personal Reflections:

Where do I go to have personal prayer time and speak directly to God, my heavenly Father? When someone asks for prayer do I immediately offer to pray, or suggest I contact a prayer chain?

_____

_____

_____

_____

_____

_____

_____

_____

_____

_____

March 8

The cares of this world are on our doorsteps every day. God's Word tells us to be anxious for nothing. As His children, we need to trust Him just as we trust in those who genuinely care for us. Exchange those anxious cares for moments of prayer *(Philippians 4:6–7)*. Let your heavenly Father know what is in your heart and on your mind. The truth He reveals to you during these times will set you free.

> Take therefore no thought for the morrow: for the morrow shall take thought for the things of itself. Sufficient unto the day is the evil thereof.
> —*Matthew 6:34*

Personal Reflections:

What is worth worrying about tomorrow, next week or even next year? Describe examples of prayer that turned out for my good when it seemed impossible at first *(Romans 8:28)*.

_____

_____

_____

_____

_____

_____

_____

_____

_____

_____

_____

March 9

God did not send His only begotten Son into this world to criticize us and point out our faults, but to rescue us from bondage. We all have sinned, so God extended His mercy and longsuffering by offering Jesus Christ to die in our place. When we judge others, we speak evil of God's creation *(James 4:12)*.

> Judge not, that ye be not judged. For with what judgment ye judge, you shall be judged: and with what measure ye mete, it shall be measured to you again.
>
> —*Matthew 7:1–2*

Personal Reflections:

What circumstances cause me to fall into the trap of judging others? How would I feel if someone judged me in the same measure in which I judge others?

_____

_____

_____

_____

_____

_____

_____

_____

_____

_____

_____

March 10

How do you want others to respond to you? Even a smile counts for something. What will you do for someone to put this verse into motion?

> Therefore all things whatsoever ye would that men should do to you, do ye even so to them: for this is the law and the prophets.
>
> —*Matthew 7:12*

Personal Reflections:

What ways do I desire to be treated? What preconceived ideas do I have that affect how I treat other people?

_____

_____

_____

_____

_____

_____

_____

_____

_____

_____

_____

_____

_____

_____

_____

March 11

Within the church, there are those among us who appear spiritually mature outwardly, but a different nature lurks on the inside. Some are ravenous wolves, and not Christ's true sheep. The Word of God warns believers that we will recognize false brethren, preachers and teachers by their fruit. We must not equate maturity or authenticity with position, length of church membership, or with whom someone associates. Outward appearances can be misleading. The Word of God and the Holy Spirit help us to know what is genuine *(1 John 4:1–6).*

> Beware of false prophets, which come to you in sheep's clothing, but inwardly they are ravening wolves. Ye shall know them by their fruits. Do men gather grapes of thorns, or figs of thistles? Even so every good tree bringeth forth good fruit; but a corrupt tree bringeth forth evil fruit.
>
> *—Matthew 7:15–17*

Personal Reflections:

How would I recognize false prophets within the church? What Bible clues would help me discern false teachers within my denomination?

_____

_____

_____

_____

_____

_____

_____

Kathe S. Rumsey & Roberta M. Wong

March 12

What a tragedy to have Jesus say, "I never knew you: depart from me, ye that work iniquity." While on earth, Jesus always obeyed the will of His heavenly Father. If we are the Lord's disciples, we must follow His example.

> Not every one that saith unto me, Lord, Lord, shall enter into the kingdom of heaven; but he that doeth the will of my Father which is in heaven. Many will say to me in that day, Lord, Lord, have we not prophesied in thy name? and in thy name cast out devils? and in thy name done many wonderful works? And then will I profess unto them, I never knew you: depart from me, ye that work iniquity.
>
> —*Matthew 7:21–23*

Personal Reflections:

How will Jesus know me when He returns? What do I hope to hear when I see Jesus in person for the first time?

_____

_____

_____

_____

_____

_____

_____

_____

_____

March 13

We maximize our life by hearing the Word of God and obeying what we hear. Life can be that straightforward.

> And every one that heareth these sayings of mine, and doeth them not, shall be likened unto a foolish man, which built his house upon the sand: and the rain descended, and the floods came, and the winds blew, and beat upon that house; and it fell: and great was the fall of it.
>
> —*Matthew 7:26–27*

Personal Reflections:

How do I think spending eternity with the foolish of this world will go? What type of foundation am I building my life upon?

_____

_____

_____

_____

_____

_____

_____

_____

_____

_____

_____

_____

_____

Kathe S. Rumsey & Roberta M. Wong

March 14

If we plan our lives by what the mainstream media reports, we would lose all hope. They attempt to indoctrinate their viewers with every wind of misinformation.

God has promised to supply all we need through Jesus Christ *(Philippians 4:19)*. The Word of God proclaims good news. Our faith in God's ability to take care of us extinguishes anxieties, doubts, and fears. Jesus Christ, the Word of God, is the same yesterday, today, and forever *(Hebrews 13:8)*.

> Why are ye fearful, O ye of little faith?
> —*Matthew 8:26*

Personal Reflections:

Why am I fearful if God did not give me a spirit of fear *(2 Timothy 1:7)*? If I desire to increase my faith, what must I do? *(Romans 10:17)*?

_____

_____

_____

_____

_____

_____

_____

_____

_____

_____

_____

March 15

When we acknowledge marriage as a covenant relationship that God ordained in the beginning, we will understand marriage as a binding agreement that includes God Himself. Marriage is a covenant agreement between a man and a woman stipulated by God *(Genesis 2:21–24; Matthew 19:6).* Since God has ordained this union for the sake of mankind, He will never alter His Word or change His position *(James 1:17).*

> It hath been said, Whosoever shall put away his wife, let him give her a writing of divorcement: but I say unto you, That whosoever shall put away his wife, saving for the cause of fornication, causeth her to commit adultery: and whosoever shall marry her that is divorced committeth adultery.
>
> *—Matthew 5:31–32*

Personal Reflections:

Describe my commitment to the marriage contract between my spouse, myself, God, and why God is the key. What options in God's eyes would I have if my marriage fell apart?

_____

_____

_____

_____

_____

_____

_____

_____

Kathe S. Rumsey & Roberta M. Wong

March 16

There is no doubt that corruption exists in every area of life; the world continues to defiantly oppose God and His goodness. Scripture instructs us to walk carefully, not as fools. We must wisely obey God's Word to redeem each day according to His plan because the days are evil. Scripture supplies all we need to fulfill His will *(2 Timothy 3:16–17)*.

> See then that ye walk circumspectly, not as fools, but as wise, redeeming the time, because the days are evil. Wherefore be ye not unwise, but understanding what the will of the Lord is.
>
> *—Ephesians 5:15–16*

Personal Reflections:

What are the signs of my will in action every day, and how does it compare to God's will? What is more important to experience: a long life, a good time in life, or to have a godly life?

_____

_____

_____

_____

_____

_____

_____

_____

_____

_____

March 17

As we celebrate Saint Patrick's Day, let us consider his life and the six years he remained imprisoned in Ireland. After Patrick escaped confinement, he returned to his homeland, England. There an angel of God spoke to him in a dream and told him to return as a missionary to Ireland. Patrick's life is an example of a Spirit-led life of obedience, fulfilling God's will. Like him, we too must have ears to hear the Holy Spirit and be willing and ready to go when and where He sends us.

> Therefore said he [Jesus] unto them, The harvest truly is great, but the laborers are few: pray ye therefore the Lord of the harvest, that he would send forth laborers into his harvest. Go your ways: behold, I send you forth as lambs among wolves.
>
> —*Luke 10:2–3*

Personal Reflections:

How do unbelievers respond to mature believers in our culture? How will God use me if I am willing to obey His direction?

_____

_____

_____

_____

_____

_____

_____

_____

_____

Kathe S. Rumsey & Roberta M. Wong

March 18

It has been said, "Luxury begins where necessity ends" (Gabrielle B. Chanel). Seeking the world's luxuries should not be the motivation behind how Christians invest our time and resources. Our lifework should be what God has purposed for us individually. He has promised to meet our needs when we seek His kingdom first *(Matthew 6:33)*. Worry and stress are not a part of God's kingdom.

> Therefore I say unto you, Take no thought for your life, what ye shall eat, or what ye shall drink; nor yet for your body, what ye shall put on. (For after all these things do the Gentiles seek:) for your heavenly Father knoweth that ye have need of all these things.
> —*Matthew 6:25, 32*

Personal Reflections:

Why do I worry about the things that have no eternal value? How do I receive my needs met from God's perspective?

_____

_____

_____

_____

_____

_____

_____

_____

_____

_____

March 19

God and His will must be first in our daily life. To love God with all our heart is to seek and know Him intimately. He desires more than a casual relationship; our Bridegroom longs for our companionship. All the wealth this world has to offer is a mere pittance compared to a lifetime with God, now and forever.

> No man can serve two masters: for either he will hate the one, and love the other; or else he will hold to the one, and despise the other. Ye cannot serve God and mammon.
>
> *—Matthew 6:24*

Personal Reflections:

How can I invest my time developing a personal relationship with God? Which relationship has greater value, one with God, or one with the world?

_____

_____

_____

_____

_____

_____

_____

_____

_____

_____

_____

_____

Kathe S. Rumsey & Roberta M. Wong

March 20

Our heavenly Father desires to have a personal relationship with us. He wants us to approach Him just as any child would draw near a gentle, loving parent. We can pour out our heart and He will listen. Jesus has made a way for us *(John 14:13–14; 15:16)*.

> But when ye pray, use not vain repetitions, as the heathen do: for they think that they shall be heard for their much speaking. Be not ye therefore like unto them: for your Father knoweth what things ye have need of, before ye ask him.
>
> *—Matthew 6:7–8*

Personal Reflections:

Have I learned to pray according to the manner in which Jesus taught His followers, or according to denominational teaching? What determines God's response to my prayers?

_____

_____

_____

_____

_____

_____

_____

_____

_____

_____

_____

_____

March 21

We can begin each day anew by seeking the Lord with all our heart. As we draw near to God, He will draw near to us *(James 4:8)*. Our heavenly Father desires only the best for each of His children. He loves us with an unconditional, everlasting love, for He is love. We must forsake ungodly ways and unrighteous thoughts. Press on and walk in God's best *(Philippians 3:13–14)*.

> Seek ye the LORD while he may be found, call ye upon him while he is near: let the wicked forsake his way, and the unrighteous man his thoughts: and let him return unto the LORD, and he will have mercy upon him; and to our God, for he will abundantly pardon.
>
> *—Isaiah 55:6–7*

Personal Reflections:

What is more beneficial: spending time with God in prayer, or rationalizing that tomorrow will be more convenient with my schedule? What kind of hold does sin have on my life?

_____

_____

_____

_____

_____

_____

_____

_____

_____

_____

Kathe S. Rumsey & Roberta M. Wong

March 22

When will we let go and allow God to direct our life? He cares more for us than we realize. He knows all things. He sees all things. As our trust in God matures, we can let go of trying to hold onto our life to control our own destiny. The more we come to know God and His nature, our trust in Him deepens *(Matthew 16:24–25)*.

> For my thoughts are not your thoughts, neither are your ways my ways, saith the Lord. For as the heavens are higher than the earth, so are my ways higher than your ways, and my thoughts than your thoughts.
> —*Isaiah 55:8–9*

Personal Reflections:

Where do I seek wisdom for my daily decisions? Would I be more comfortable solving my own problems, or asking God for help?

_____

_____

_____

_____

_____

_____

_____

_____

_____

_____

_____

March 23

The deeper our relationship with the Lord Jesus Christ becomes, the more we hunger for the time we can spend in His presence. The world around us becomes emptier, less fulfilling, and no longer satisfies our thirst for all that God created us to experience. Each day is a new opportunity to seek God. Do not miss an opportunity.

> O GOD, thou art my God; early will I seek thee: my soul thirsteth for thee, my flesh longeth for thee in a dry and thirsty land, where no water is; to see thy power and thy glory, so as I have seen thee in the sanctuary.
>
> —*Psalm 63:1–2*

Personal Reflections:

In addition to the cares of this world, what drains the joy out of my life? How can I bring the joy, power, and glory of God back into my inner being?

_____

_____

_____

_____

_____

_____

_____

_____

_____

Kathe S. Rumsey & Roberta M. Wong

March 24

Through his personal testimony, we learn that Paul endured persecutions, afflictions, shipwrecks, beatings and imprisonments, to name a few. He said, "But thou hast fully known my doctrine, manner of life, purpose, faith, longsuffering, charity, patience" *(2 Timothy 3:10)*. Because of Paul's life of faith, we can trust what he says. He counsels us to follow his example and the God of peace will be with us.

> Those things, which ye have both learned, and received, and heard, and seen in me, do: and the God of peace shall be with you.
>
> —*Philippians 4:9*

Personal Reflections:

How do I achieve God's peace in my life? Just as Apostle Paul endured grievous trials in this world and experienced the peace of God, how can I truly find God's peace in the things I suffer?

_____

_____

_____

_____

_____

_____

_____

_____

_____

_____

_____

March 25

All around us we see pride and arrogance flaunted in the face of righteousness. As we honor the Lord, those things that are an abomination to Him will become repugnant to us. Christians must guard against the seductions and deceptions of the world. We must live our life based upon the truth of God's Word. He has promised to provide His wisdom liberally to all *(James 1:5)*.

> I wisdom dwell with prudence, and find out knowledge of witty inventions. The fear of the LORD is to hate evil: pride, and arrogancy, and the evil way, and the froward [perverse] mouth, do I hate.
>
> —*Proverbs 8:12–13*

Personal Reflections:

What can I do to honor God in the midst of the evil that permeates society? How long will God tolerate the things that bring out a prideful spirit in me?

March 26

God so loved the world that He sent His only begotten Son Jesus Christ to save it *(John 3:16)*. Yet a perishing world rejects Him. To build a life upon contemporary world systems and its capricious wisdom is fruitless. None of these will endure; they are temporary. If you could change only one thing, what would you do differently? Without Christ, we can do nothing *(John 15:5)*.

> Jesus answered and said unto him, If a man love me, he will keep my words: and my Father will love him, and we will come unto him, and make our abode with him. He that loveth me not keepeth not my sayings: and the word which ye hear is not mine, but the Father's which sent me.
>
> *—John 14:23–24*

Personal Reflections:

What should be my perspective when God closes doors in my life? What am I willing to exchange for the opportunity to follow Jesus Christ?

_____

_____

_____

_____

_____

_____

_____

_____

March 27

Daily we face challenges at home, at work, and at school. God promises to give us His wisdom to meet these trials successfully. Faith in our Lord and Savior Jesus Christ, the Word of God, equips us to overcome whatever comes our way. No matter how inadequate we feel or believe ourselves to be, God will never express disapproval as we humbly seek His help. He will abundantly supply us with what we need to know.

> If any of you lack wisdom, let him ask of God, that giveth to all men liberally, and upbraideth not; and it shall be given him. But let him ask in faith, nothing wavering. For he that wavereth is like a wave of the sea driven with the wind and tossed. For let not that man think that he shall receive any thing of the Lord. A double minded man is unstable in all his ways.
>
> —*James 1:5–8*

Personal Reflections:

In a society that touts having all the answers, where can I find godly solutions for the challenges I face? When I do not like the doors God opens for me, should I rely upon my own wisdom?

_____

_____

_____

_____

_____

_____

_____

Kathe S. Rumsey & Roberta M. Wong

March 28

The world has become a whirligig of events. We are in perpetual motion, going around and around, back and forth, only to wish all the madness would cease. There is no peace, no rest, no joy, no fulfillment nor satisfaction in what we do. Is it any wonder why? Life is upside-down, in constant change, and yet unfulfilling. How can we make choices that will honor God?

> If thou turn away thy foot from the sabbath, from doing thy pleasure on my holy day; and call the sabbath a delight, the holy of the LORD, honorable; and shalt honor him, not doing thine own ways, nor finding thine own pleasure, nor speaking thine own words: then shalt thou delight thyself in the LORD; and I will cause thee to ride upon the high places of the earth, and feed thee with the heritage of Jacob thy father: for the mouth of the LORD hath spoken it.
>
> —*Isaiah 58:13–14*

Personal Reflections:

How do I choose to spend my sabbath, and with whom? How can I make changes in my lifestyle to accommodate a higher calling than I currently live?

_____

_____

_____

_____

_____

_____

March 29

The body of Christ has the talent needed to accomplish every task God has planned for our lives. How should we meet the needs of others? As you pray, ask the Lord what He would have you do to assist others within your congregation and community. As the Holy Spirit leads, invite other Christians to join you.

> Be kindly affectioned one to another with brotherly love; in honor preferring one another; not slothful in business; fervent in spirit; serving the Lord; rejoicing in hope; patient in tribulation; continuing instant in prayer; distributing to the necessity of saints; given to hospitality.
>
> —*Romans 12:10–13*

Personal Reflections:

How can I be productive and hospitable at work, while allowing my lifestyle to be a witness? What actions do I take toward those of faith?

_____

_____

_____

_____

_____

_____

_____

_____

_____

_____

March 30

The world busies itself with the acquisition and accumulation of things. Trends are here one day and gone the next, but God's Word remains eternal. If we commit our way to the Lord and make the kingdom of God and His righteousness our priority, He has promised to meet our every need *(Matthew 6:33)*.

> Wherefore, if God so clothe the grass of the field, which today is, and tomorrow is cast into the oven, shall he not much more clothe you, O ye of little faith? Therefore take no thought, saying, What shall we eat? or, What shall we drink? or, Wherewithal shall we be clothed? (For after all these things do the Gentiles seek:) for your heavenly Father knoweth that ye have need of all these things.
>
> *—Matthew 6:30–32*

Personal Reflections:

What have I learned from past experience that builds my trust in my heavenly Father's desire to meet my needs? What desires do I have in common with those who have not accepted Christ?

_____

_____

_____

_____

_____

_____

_____

_____

March 31

The Word of God is holy. Some people have a heart unreceptive to what God has for them. Therefore, we are to go only where He sends us and speak only as the Holy Spirit directs. Jesus never spoke or acted outside of the will of the Father *(John 5:19, 30; 12:49; 14:10).* If we seek God's wisdom first, we can spare ourselves so much.

> Give not that which is holy unto the dogs, neither cast
> ye your pearls before swine, lest they trample them
> under their feet, and turn again and rend you.
>
> *—Matthew 7:6*

Personal Reflections:

Should I share the good news of Jesus Christ with everyone with whom I come into contact? Describe how God has opened doors for me to share His Word.

_____

_____

_____

_____

_____

_____

_____

_____

_____

_____

_____

April 1

As believers in Jesus Christ, it is time to grow up and stop living by what we see and how we feel. It is time to be led by the Spirit of God and live by the word (rhema) we hear from Him *(Romans 10:17)*. Scripture tells us that only the wise will be ready when Jesus returns for His bride *(Matthew 25:6–13)*. Who would want to be counted among the foolish? *(Ecclesiastes 7:5)*.

> The fear of the LORD is the beginning of knowledge: but fools despise wisdom and instruction. My son, if sinners entice thee, consent thou not.
>
> —*Proverbs 1:7, 10*

Personal Reflections:

What is the hidden cause that might draw me into a sinner's trap? How do I seek wisdom and instruction from the Holy Spirit of God?

_____

_____

_____

_____

_____

_____

_____

_____

_____

_____

April 2

Christians must not engage in foolish debates regarding the Word of God *(2 Timothy 3:16)*. The Holy Spirit of God, the Spirit of truth, teaches and reveals the meaning of the Bible to us and imparts understanding *(John 16:13; 1 John 2:27)*. Many foolish questions and disputes about truth occur when we lack knowledge of God's Word in its intended context.

Our personal opinions and thoughts mean nothing. When we find ourselves in conversations with others who want to question or debate Scripture, we can be confident in the Holy Spirit to lead us into all truth. Speak only as He leads.

> But avoid foolish questions, and genealogies, and contentions, and strivings about the law; for they are unprofitable and vain. A man that is a heretic after the first and second admonition reject; knowing that he that is such is subverted, and sinneth, being condemned of himself.
>
> *—Titus 3:9–11*

Personal Reflections:

How do I respond to individuals who are divisive (heretics) even if they are family or friends? What might happen if I admonish them once, even twice, before I reject them?

Kathe S. Rumsey & Roberta M. Wong

April 3

Christian supervisors in the workplace are responsible to lead by the principles of God's Word. When we no longer esteem our employees' contributions, we have lost our godly perspective. We fail to understand the personal impact of unemployment.

Even though we may be accountable for the company's financial stability, we must not casually promote layoffs for the sake of salvaging the bottom line. God's Word will provide us with the wisdom needed when difficult situations arise.

> Masters, give unto your servants that which is just and equal; knowing that ye also have a Master in heaven.
> —*Colossians 4:1*

Personal Reflections:

If I supervise others at work, how should I treat each one of my employees? How has God, as my example of a perfect Master, been a witness to me?

April 4

Christian employees in the workplace must consider their bosses as deserving all respect. If coworkers consistently communicate among themselves in destructive or negative ways, we must not participate *(Colossians 4:5–6)*.

If you have taken part in a boss-bashing conversation, repent. Pray and ask God to help you understand why He ordained your boss for such a season and place. Take a stand for God's truth; a company divided against itself will fall *(Luke 11:17)*.

> Let as many servants as are under the yoke count their own masters worthy of all honor, that the name of God and his doctrine be not blasphemed.
>
> *—1 Timothy 6:1*

Personal Reflections:

How can I show my boss sincere respect at work? When my boss and other employees see me, what examples of godly character do they observe in me on a consistent basis?

April 5

Scripture explicitly warns us that trusting in this world's wealth can corrupt our faith and draw us away from God *(1 Timothy 6:9–10)*. We must trust in the living God who is always present and mindful of us. The true riches that bless our lives humble those who trust in God Almighty to meet their needs *(Psalm 84:12; James 4:6)*.

> Charge them that are rich in this world, that they be not highminded; nor trust in uncertain riches, but in the living God, who giveth us richly all things to enjoy.
>
> *—1 Timothy 6:17*

Personal Reflections:

How do I respond to the blessings God bestows upon me? What might I say to others to help them avoid placing their trust in the uncertain riches of this world?

_____

_____

_____

_____

_____

_____

_____

_____

_____

_____

_____

April 6

Jesus is the King of kings. He is the Lord of lords. Where His Word is, there is true power. When we face life's decisions, we will find our answers in the Word of God. His infallible Word in Ecclesiastes tells us that if we keep His commands, we will experience the benefits of our salvation. The gospel exhorts us to be doers of the Word and not hearers only, otherwise we deceive ourselves *(James 1:22)*. Our comfort and authority are in God's Word and His Word only.

> Where the word of a king is, there is power: and who
> may say unto him, What doest thou? Whoso keepeth
> the commandment shall feel no evil thing: and a wise
> man's heart discerneth both time and judgment.
> —*Ecclesiastes 8:4–5*

Personal Reflections:

In what ways have I fed my faith with the most powerful source of truth on earth, God's Word? What will I do differently if I wish to be wise from God's perspective?

_____

_____

_____

_____

_____

_____

_____

_____

Kathe S. Rumsey & Roberta M. Wong

April 7

From the moment the shout, the voice of the archangel and the trumpet of God sound, we will forever be with the Lord Jesus Christ. We, the church, must have spiritual ears to hear the Holy Spirit of God to be ready. To spend eternity with God is a breathtaking truth. Daily, we must continue to mature in our relationship with the One who truly loves us, Jesus Christ. Each of us has only one lifetime to get ready.

> For the Lord himself shall descend from heaven with a shout, with the voice of the archangel, and with the trump of God: and the dead in Christ shall rise first: then we which are alive and remain shall be caught up together with them in the clouds to meet the Lord in the air: and so shall we ever be with the Lord.
>
> *—1 Thessalonians 4:16–17*

Personal Reflections:

What must I do to be ready for our Lord's return? What makes the difference between the wise and foolish virgins in *Matthew 25:1-13?*

_____

_____

_____

_____

_____

_____

_____

April 8

As the end of the age of grace approaches, confusion and loneliness have become the norm *(2 Timothy 3:1–4)*. The chaos that surrounds us must not become a distraction or hindrance. We must remain focused on the things of God.

Those born of God are never alone. If we experience loneliness, it may be that we have focused on ourselves rather than others. No matter who disappoints or rejects us, Jesus loves us unconditionally. Faithful and true, Christ remains with us even unto the end *(Revelation 19:11)*.

> And Jesus came and spake unto them, saying, … I am with you always, even unto the end of the world [age]. Amen.
>
> *—Matthew 28:18, 20*

Personal Reflections:

What influence does the spirit of fear use to control my life? Do I confidently trust Jesus when He says He will be with me even to the end of this age, and how does this free me daily?

_____

_____

_____

_____

_____

_____

_____

_____

Kathe S. Rumsey & Roberta M. Wong

April 9

Apart from Jesus, we can do nothing *(John 6:44; 15:5)*. As the Holy Spirit leads, we are to minister God the Father's unconditional love and good news to others.

> Go ye therefore, and teach all nations, baptizing them in the name of the Father, and of the Son, and of the Holy Ghost: teaching them to observe all things whatsoever I have commanded you.
>
> *—Matthew 28:19–20*

Personal Reflections:

What can I do to be a part of teaching all nations? What part has God asked me to accomplish in His eternal plan?

_____

_____

_____

_____

_____

_____

_____

_____

_____

_____

_____

_____

_____

_____

April 10

The world exhibits its contempt of God, condemning His Son Jesus Christ. Yet it was God's love that motivated Him to send His only begotten Son into the world. Through the sacrifice of Jesus, God intended to rescue a dying world and offer eternal life *(John 3:16–17)*. His will is that none should perish. Pray for those who do not know Jesus Christ that they may be saved *(Mathew 9:38; Romans 10:9–10)*.

> And this is the condemnation, that light is come into the world, and men loved darkness rather than light, because their deeds were evil. For every one that doeth evil hateth the light, neither cometh to the light, lest his deeds should be reproved.
>
> *—John 3:16–17, 19–20*

Personal Reflections:

How do I feel when I am in the light, or in darkness? How should I interact with people of the world who prefer darkness because their deeds are evil?

April 11

Scripture teaches us that Christians are the righteousness of God through faith in Jesus Christ our Lord *(Romans 5:19)*. The Holy Spirit will instruct and guide us into all truth *(John 16:13)*. Through His guidance, we will avoid the pitfalls of compromise and deceptive traps that can so easily ensnare us. Christians are not to imitate the ways of the world. God promises to be a Father to us and we are His sons and daughters.

> Be ye not unequally yoked together with unbelievers: for what fellowship hath righteousness with unrighteousness? and what communion hath light with darkness? Wherefore come out from among them, and be ye separate, saith the Lord, and touch not the unclean thing; and I will receive you, and will be a Father unto you, and ye shall be my sons and daughters, saith the Lord Almighty.
>
> *—2 Corinthians 6:14, 17–18*

Personal Reflections:

How do my friends walk: as believers, or unbelievers? How should I participate in relationships with others if they foolishly choose to live in darkness rather than God's light?

_____

_____

_____

_____

_____

_____

April 12

Everything in this world is temporary. Even the afflictions we endure are momentary in comparison to our eternal inheritance. We must not grow weary in well doing, for we will reap a harvest in God's perfect time. Rejoice and look up. Smile. God's love for us is the same yesterday, today and forever. It is eternal.

> Therefore we do not lose heart. Even though our outward man is perishing, yet the inward man is being renewed day by day. For our light affliction, which is but for a moment, is working for us a far more exceeding and eternal weight of glory, while we do not look at the things which are seen, but at the things which are not seen. For the things which are seen are temporary, but the things which are not seen are eternal.
>
> *—2 Corinthians 4:16–18 (NKJV)*

Personal Reflections:

What causes me to feel as though I am physically under attack from all sides? In comparison to eternity, how would I equate the difficulties and uncertainties in my life?

_____

_____

_____

_____

_____

_____

_____

Kathe S. Rumsey & Roberta M. Wong

April 13

Jesus paid a high price for our redemption. Let us esteem His work with the highest regard. Even when we do not fully grasp all aspects of our salvation, we must not treat it with casual consideration. We owe Him everything. We can never repay Him. What does your salvation mean to you?

> We then, as workers together with him, beseech you also that ye receive not the grace of God in vain. (For he saith, I have heard thee in a time accepted, and in the day of salvation have I succored [helped] thee: behold, now is the accepted time; behold, now is the day of salvation.)
>
> —*2 Corinthians 6:1–2*

Personal Reflections:

What makes me confident of my salvation? If Jesus provides my salvation by grace, and grace alone, why would I feel I have to earn it by my works?

_____

_____

_____

_____

_____

_____

_____

_____

_____

April 14

Church, wake up! The hour is late. We must be ready *(Revelation 19:7)*.

> But I [Jesus] have a few things against thee, because thou hast there them that hold the doctrine of Balaam, who taught Balak to cast a stumblingblock before the children of Israel, to eat things sacrificed unto idols, and to commit fornication. So hast thou also them that hold the doctrine of the Nicolaitanes, which thing I hate. Repent; or else I will come unto thee quickly, and will fight against them with the sword of my mouth. He that hast an ear, let him hear what the Spirit saith unto the churches.
>
> *—Revelation 2:14–17*

Personal Reflections:

Why do I compromise with the world and allow things God hates to become part of His church? What should I do when I see the church compromising to fit in with the world's programs?

_____

_____

_____

_____

_____

_____

_____

_____

_____

Kathe S. Rumsey & Roberta M. Wong

April 15

It impossible to serve both God and mammon. Under our current tax laws, we are legally entitled to certain monetary advantages. However, some Christians deceitfully misuse the law seeking loopholes, thinking they are wise. As God's children, we must not compromise our integrity to save a few dollars. Jesus said, "Render therefore unto Caesar the things which be Caesar's, and unto God the things which be God's" *(Luke 20:25).*

> So teach us to number our days, that we may apply our hearts unto wisdom.
>
> *—Psalm 90:12*

Personal Reflections:

How can I redeem the time I have to walk in God's wisdom? Explain how I would prioritize my life if this was to be my last day before meeting Jesus Christ in person.

_____

_____

_____

_____

_____

_____

_____

_____

_____

_____

_____

April 16

As we establish our relationships with God first, and then with others, a fellowship of trust follows. This provides an environment to speak the truth in love and allows the Holy Spirit to operate in our midst. We are free to encourage one another to be faithful servants to Christ. We must learn what commitment means to God. Our yes should be yes; no should be no *(James 5:12)*.

> But exhort one another daily, while it is called Today; lest any of you be hardened through the deceitfulness of sin. For we are made partakers of Christ, if we hold the beginning of our confidence steadfast unto the end.
>
> *—Hebrews 3:13–14*

Personal Reflections:

What should I do to ensure I do not fall prey to the deceitfulness of sin? How can I best exhort others?

_____

_____

_____

_____

_____

_____

_____

_____

_____

_____

Kathe S. Rumsey & Roberta M. Wong

April 17

Jesus Christ's love for all people is unconditional and sacrificial. Only when we release our past are we free to receive the future God has for us. The body of Christ needs one another *(1 Corinthians 12:18–23; Colossians 3:8–16).*

> And grieve not the Holy Spirit of God, whereby ye are sealed unto the day of redemption. Let all bitterness, and wrath, and anger, and clamor, and evil speaking, be put away from you, with all malice: and be ye kind to one another, tenderhearted, forgiving one another, even as God for Christ's sake hath forgiven you.
>
> *—Ephesians 4:30–32*

Personal Reflections:

Explain how I respond to people who let the flood of bitterness flow out of their mouth toward me. What comes out of my mouth when I get frustrated?

_____

_____

_____

_____

_____

_____

_____

_____

_____

_____

April 18

Time is our most valued commodity, prized more than gold. As wise followers of Christ, we focus on God's will in order to be ready for Jesus' arrival *(1 Thessalonians 4:15–18)*. We make certain that we have oil in our vessels with our lamps *(Matthew 25:1–13)*. We remain vigilant and do not allow the world to influence our decisions. The Lamb's wife is getting herself ready *(Revelation 19:7)*.

> See then that ye walk circumspectly, not as fools, but as wise, redeeming the time, because the days are evil. Wherefore be ye not unwise, but understanding what the will of the Lord is.
>
> *—Ephesians 5:15–17*

Personal Reflections:

When everyone is spewing lies, how can I walk wisely in truth redeeming the time? What is my source for understanding the will of God?

_____

_____

_____

_____

_____

_____

_____

_____

_____

Kathe S. Rumsey & Roberta M. Wong

April 19

These days, more children routinely disrespect their parents and the elderly, evidenced by media reports. Naively, generations are racing down a path of self-destruction.

God's laws operate perpetually regardless of our ignorance of them. No matter what age we may be, we are to honor our father and mother whether deserved or not.

> Honor thy father and mother; which is the first commandment with promise; that it may be well with thee, and thou mayest live long on the earth.
>
> —*Ephesians 6:2–3*

Personal Reflections:

Describe why it does not matter if my father or mother deserve honor. What does God expect from me in regard to my parents?

_____

_____

_____

_____

_____

_____

_____

_____

_____

_____

_____

_____

_____

April 20

The inscription on the United States of America's currency, *In God We Trust*, is her official motto. Ironically, some of our country's citizens challenge any reference to God in the public domain.

If our nation's enemies from within cannot remove *In God We Trust* from our currency, then they will seek a way to replace our money with a one-world monetary system. We must pray for our nation and its leaders. Once again, we need God's intervention to restore America before it is too late *(2 Chronicles 7:14)*.

> Blessed is the nation whose God is the LORD.
>
> —*Psalm 33:12*

Personal Reflections:

Explain why it matters if a nation's governing body honors God as LORD. What are the consequences for a nation and its people that reject God?

_____

_____

_____

_____

_____

_____

_____

_____

_____

_____

_____

_____

_____

Kathe S. Rumsey & Roberta M. Wong

April 21

Thank God for the friends He has placed in your life. True friends exhort one another with His truth and encourage with His unconditional love. Our interactions with other believers sharpen our understanding of the Word of God. Be eternally grateful for these relationships. They are priceless!

> Iron sharpeneth iron; so a man sharpeneth the countenance of his friend.
> —*Proverbs 27:17*

Personal Reflections:

What can I do to help my friends walk even closer with God? What could my friends do to help me remain consistent in my walk with God?

_____

_____

_____

_____

_____

_____

_____

_____

_____

_____

_____

_____

April 22

Do you have a friend who loves you unconditionally? Are you the type of friend who loves others unconditionally? When we love others with God's love which is without conditions, we are unable to be offended. Family and friends are the mortar that holds the bricks of life together in adversity. Jesus Christ is our chief cornerstone *(1 Peter 2:6)*.

> A friend loveth at all times, and a brother is born for adversity.
>
> *—Proverbs 17:17*

Personal Reflections:

Describe how I can demonstrate my trustworthiness toward friends who are faithful no matter what happens. Explain how I can make myself available when a brother suffers misfortune.

_____

_____

_____

_____

_____

_____

_____

_____

_____

_____

_____

_____

Kathe S. Rumsey & Roberta M. Wong

April 23

As we learn to submit to Christ as head in all situations, it reinforces our faith. We will no longer depend upon personal experience alone, but trust in the wisdom the Holy Spirit supplies in God's Word. Our reliance upon Jesus teaches us to trust Him with our whole heart, no matter what we see around us. When we put this verse into practice, we will experience God's peace and strength in our lives.

> Trust in the LORD with all thine heart; and lean not unto thine own understanding. In all thy ways acknowledge him, and he shall direct thy paths.
>
> —*Proverbs 3:5–6*

Personal Reflections:

What does it mean for me to trust in the LORD with all my heart? How can I develop patience to wait for God to direct my paths?

_____

_____

_____

_____

_____

_____

_____

_____

_____

_____

_____

_____

April 24

If you are currently dissatisfied with your job, roll the concern of it onto God. Trust Him to make the necessary changes to establish you, no matter where you are or whatever you do. The best place to be is in the center of His will. If unemployed, seek God's direction for your next position.

> Commit thy works unto the LORD, and thy thoughts shall be established.
>
> —*Proverbs 16:3*

Personal Reflections:

How do I stop trying to figure everything out, and begin to give my concerns over to God? What will I need to change in order for me to completely trust God with my life?

_____

_____

_____

_____

_____

_____

_____

_____

_____

_____

_____

_____

_____

April 25

As Christians, we must not conform to the trends and lifestyles of this present age. When we feel pressured to condone its immorality, or obey its mandated norms of speech and behavior, we must remember who we are in Christ. We are in this world, but not of it.

A chaotic, unrestrained world view continues to erode our nation's godly foundation *(1 John 2:15)*. The Ten Commandments will forever remain God's standard for mankind, whether we choose to live by them, or not.

> If my people, which are called by my name, shall humble themselves, and pray, and seek my face, and turn from their wicked ways; then will I hear from heaven, and will forgive their sin, and will heal their land.
>
> *—2 Chronicles 7:14*

Personal Reflections:

Explain what I am prepared to do in order for God to heal the country where I reside. What would I be willing to change if my life does not please God?

_____

_____

_____

_____

_____

_____

_____

_____

April 26

Insecurity, jealousy, and envy breed gossip. In our current society, it is the most destructive form of communication. Gossip, intertwined with slander, destroys lives; widespread like cancer in some congregations, it destroys unity and harmony.

Gossip and slander are evil violations against other human beings. Our world carelessly views this form of communication with casual regard, even as entertainment. However, know this, to God, it is an abomination *(Proverbs 6:16–19)*.

> He that covereth a transgression seeketh love; but he
> that repeateth a matter separateth very friends.
>
> *—Proverbs 17:9*

Personal Reflections:

Describe why it is important to be a true friend. How can I stop the flow of negative words in my sphere of influence?

_____

_____

_____

_____

_____

_____

_____

_____

_____

_____

_____

April 27

Everyone will experience temptations, without exception. However, God assures us that He will not allow us to be tempted beyond what we are able to endure. Our confidence in His Word enables us to withstand evil on any given day *(Ephesians 6:13; James 4:7).*

> There hath no temptation taken you but such as is common to man: but God is faithful, who will not suffer you to be tempted above that ye are able; but will with the temptation also make a way to escape, that ye may be able to bear it.
>
> *—1 Corinthians 10:13*

Personal Reflections:

Describe how I should react when temptations come against me. How has God led me out of a tempting situation in the past?

_____

_____

_____

_____

_____

_____

_____

_____

_____

_____

_____

_____

April 28

If Jesus were to return this morning, where would He find you? What would He find you doing? Would you behave differently toward others? Would you make different choices than those made yesterday? Live as though His return comes before sunset. Choose life!

> For all that is in the world, the lust of the flesh, and the lust of the eyes, and the pride of life, is not of the Father, but is of the world. And now, little children, abide in him, that, when he shall appear, we may have confidence, and not be ashamed before him at his coming.
>
> —*1 John 2:16, 28*

Personal Reflections:

Describe how I expect to be living when Jesus returns for His bride. What makes me confident that when I stand before Jesus, I will have lived the life He planned for me?

_____

_____

_____

_____

_____

_____

_____

_____

_____

_____

Kathe S. Rumsey & Roberta M. Wong

April 29

Sin is deceptive; it can creep into our lives unaware. How we occupy our time is important; do we live wisely or foolishly? Where do we go to enrich our lives? What do we watch on television or at the movies, and with whom do we spend our time? Even church activities that seem harmless can be contrary to God's will for us. We must stay alert. Watch and pray *(Matthew 26:41).*

> Beloved, now are we the sons of God, and it doeth not
> yet appear what we shall be: but we know that, when
> he shall appear, we shall be like him; for we shall see
> him as he is. And every man that hath this hope in
> him purifieth himself, even as he [Jesus] is pure. Little
> children, keep yourselves from idols. Amen.
>
> *—1 John 3:2–3; 5:21*

Personal Reflections:

What will I be busy doing when the *catching away*, the *rapture* takes place? How can I make sure I am preparing daily for Jesus' return, and what should I be doing differently?

_____

_____

_____

_____

_____

_____

_____

_____

April 30

The bride, the Lamb's wife, will spend eternity with her beloved Bridegroom Jesus Christ. Each one of us has only one lifetime to get ourselves ready *(1 Thessalonians 4:16–17)*.

> Let us be glad and rejoice, and give honor to him: for the marriage of the Lamb is come, and his wife hath made herself ready.
>
> —*Revelation 19:7*

Personal Reflections:

How can believers help one another to prepare for Jesus' return? How will I know Jesus has returned for His bride if I am not prepared?

May 1

There is coming a time when the voice of Jesus Christ and His bride will vanish. When this happens, the nations of the world will rejoice because they have been deceived. Without cause, they hated and rejected God's Son Jesus and everything He freely offered. Pray the Lord of the harvest to send laborers into His field. Ask the Holy Spirit to bring someone into your life that needs to know Jesus Christ as his or her Lord and Savior. The Day of salvation is too valuable to waste.

> And the light of a candle shall shine no more at all in thee; and the voice of the bridegroom and of the bride shall be heard no more at all in thee: for thy merchants were the great men of the earth; for by thy sorceries were all nations deceived.
> —*Revelation 18:23*

Personal Reflections:

What does it mean to be ready when the Bridegroom comes? What would cause Jesus to shut the door and say He never knew me?

_____

_____

_____

_____

_____

_____

_____

_____

May 2

Jesus Christ is the Son of God. He is the creator and heir of all things, visible and invisible. He is the Bridegroom who paid the price for our redemption. Do you know this man Jesus? Do you know Him well enough to feel comfortable at His side for eternity? *(Revelation 19:7)*. Draw near to God and He will draw near to you *(James 4:8)*.

> God, who at various times and in different ways spoke in time past to the fathers by the prophets, has in these last days spoken to us by His Son, whom He has appointed heir of all things, through whom also He made the worlds.
>
> *—Hebrews 1:1–2 (NKJV)*

Personal Reflections:

Have I made myself ready for the arrival of Jesus Christ? Describe what the season will be like when it is time for His return.

_____

_____

_____

_____

_____

_____

_____

_____

_____

_____

May 3

Eternal life begins the moment we accept Jesus Christ as our Lord and Savior. Immediately, we become citizens of the kingdom of heaven and heirs of the throne. The opportunity to inherit all the promises of God belongs to us. What good news!

> Verily, verily, I say unto you, He that heareth my word, and believeth on him that sent me, hath everlasting life, and shall not come into condemnation; but is passed from death unto life.
>
> —*John 5:24*

Personal Reflections:

What is the indicator that I have passed from death unto life? Describe what makes me confident in my personal relationship with Jesus Christ, the King of kings.

_____

_____

_____

_____

_____

_____

_____

_____

_____

_____

_____

_____

May 4

Some in our workplace bless us with their words, but curse us inwardly. Some compliment us only in the presence of others from whom they are seeking approval. Like a deceitful cloak of friendship, these accolades come from a false heart. However, if a true friend speaks words that pierce us, we can trust that these wounds are for our benefit.

> Faithful are the wounds of a friend; but the kisses of an enemy are deceitful.
>
> —*Proverbs 27:6*

Personal Reflections:

Why would I choose the wounds of a friend over the kisses of an enemy? What do the words *faithful wounds* and *deceitful kisses* actually mean in Hebrew and English?

_____

_____

_____

_____

_____

_____

_____

_____

_____

_____

_____

May 5

When others appear to be successful and move up the career ladder with ease, all the while stepping on everyone who gets in their way, do not join forces with the unrighteous. Pray and seek God's secret counsel. He knows the plans He has for you.

> Envy thou not the oppressor, and choose none of his
> ways. For the froward is abomination to the LORD: but
> his secret is with the righteous.
> —*Proverbs 3:31–32*

Personal Reflections:

Describe my understanding of the plans God has for me to accomplish. How can I avoid feelings of jealousy smoldering within me when schemers are promoted in the workplace?

_____

_____

_____

_____

_____

_____

_____

_____

_____

_____

_____

_____

_____

May 6

What could be more wonderful than life created and planned by God Almighty? If we stumble, it changes nothing. Get up, repent, and continue to follow Jesus through the strait gate and narrow way *(Matthew 7:14)*. He is our faithful Shepherd *(Psalm 37:23)*.

> Though he fall, he shall not be utterly cast down: for the Lord upholdeth him with his hand.
>
> *—Psalm 37:24*

Personal Reflections:

Will God walk away from me if I am not a perfect Christian? What does true repentance require of me?

_____

_____

_____

_____

_____

_____

_____

_____

_____

_____

_____

_____

_____

_____

_____

_____

_____

May 7

It is easy to become lukewarm when we compromise and allow our life to drift with the currents of this world and its cultures. When was the last time you were truly on fire for God—a time when He was the main priority of your day—a time when you lived just to pray and be alone with Him?

Redeem your time today to be alone with your heavenly Father. A single word from Him will ignite your courage to withstand the influences of evil. Stand strong. Fight the good fight of faith.

> I [Jesus] know thy works, that thou art neither cold nor hot: I would thou wast cold or hot. So then because thou art lukewarm, and neither cold nor hot, I will spew thee out of my mouth.
>
> *—Revelation 3:15–16*

Personal Reflections:

Have I given into compromise so long that I have now become nauseating to God? What must I do to reignite my passion for God and His Word?

_____

_____

_____

_____

_____

_____

_____

_____

May 8

Some Christians refer to *John 14:2* in a worldly application, as though it is a promise of riches and mansions fashioned out of Hollywood photographs. Jesus is not a general contractor who left earth to design and build an opulent castle in the sky. Because of our relationship with Jesus Christ, the King of kings, worldly wealth loses its appeal. The kingdom of God far excels anything comparable this world offers in exchange.

> And if I go and prepare a place for you, I will come again, and receive you unto myself; that where I am, there ye may be also.
>
> *—John 14:3*

Personal Reflections:

Describe how I will be ready when Jesus returns for His bride. Describe anything in my life that keeps me in bondage to the lifestyle I presently lead.

_____

_____

_____

_____

_____

_____

_____

_____

_____

_____

Kathe S. Rumsey & Roberta M. Wong

May 9

When a boss lacks the necessary skills to plan effectively thereby creating a chaotic and stressful environment, how should Christians respond? What if a manager constantly targets his employees to fail; how can we handle this situation to ensure a more favorable outcome? There may be times when deadlines to complete insignificant details override the critical issues of the workplace.

Christians face a variety of challenges daily. If we respond with integrity to our boss and other employees, with God's help, we can place these burdens on His shoulders. The Holy Spirit will guide us.

> Masters, give unto your servants that which is just and equal; knowing that ye also have a Master in heaven.
> —*Colossians 4:1*

Personal Reflections:

If I supervise others in the workplace, how would they describe me as a boss? Explain what I could do differently to eliminate frustration and stress for my employees.

_____
_____
_____
_____
_____
_____
_____
_____

May 10

If we truly follow Christ, then we will walk in godly wisdom. We will make our decisions based upon the knowledge the Holy Spirit of God supplies through the Word. This is true wisdom *(Proverbs 4:1–27; 1 Corinthians 1:24).*

How did Jesus treat those outside the Jewish community? He never judged others. His love was unconditional and still is. When people witnessed how Jesus responded to others, they knew they had encountered someone truly remarkable.

> Walk in wisdom toward them that are without, redeeming the time.
>
> *—Colossians 4:5*

Personal Reflections:

Explain how I could share my faith with those who do not have faith. Describe a time when I have asked God to give me wisdom and the words to share with an unbeliever, and what resulted.

_____

_____

_____

_____

_____

_____

_____

_____

_____

_____

Kathe S. Rumsey & Roberta M. Wong

May 11

This moment may be the last opportunity to represent Truth here on earth. Our lives should reflect God's nature, and not our own. If we redeem the earliest part of our day in prayer and seek God's wisdom, we will be better equipped to withstand the day's challenges.

> See then that ye walk circumspectly, not as fools, but
> as wise, redeeming the time, because the days are evil.
> —*Ephesians 5:15–16*

Personal Reflections:

Describe the depth of evil that is lurking all around me whether at work, or in my nation. How can I be wise, and redeem the opportunities God opens for me to shed light in these situations?

_____

_____

_____

_____

_____

_____

_____

_____

_____

_____

_____

_____

_____

May 12

As God's servants, we must be careful not to put a stumbling block before others in anything. Our service for Christ, whether it is practical or spiritual, must not be undermined by selfish actions *(2 Corinthians 6:1–18)*. If our eye be single, our whole body will be full of light *(Matthew 6:22)*.

> We give no offense in anything, that our ministry may not be blamed.
>
> —*2 Corinthians 6:3 (NKJV)*

Personal Reflections:

How can I be faithful in eliminating stumbling blocks and sin from my own life? Describe how others might recognize the nature of Jesus when they observe my lifestyle.

_____

_____

_____

_____

_____

_____

_____

_____

_____

_____

_____

_____

_____

May 13

God's kingdom does not operate like the world's kingdoms. He is not Uncle Sam. He does not require or need a tax from the body of Christ to fulfill His will on earth. God delights in is a cheerful giver, one who freely meets the true needs of others and does not live in bondage to the things of this world. May our giving be out of a pure heart *(2 Corinthians 9:6)*.

> Every man according as he purposeth in his heart, so let him give; not grudgingly, or of necessity: for God loveth a cheerful giver.
>
> *—2 Corinthians 9:7*

Personal Reflections:

Explain why I give donations to my church denomination. How have I sought the Holy Spirit's leading as to what and where to give?

_____

_____

_____

_____

_____

_____

_____

_____

_____

_____

_____

May 14

When God has a work for us to do, He provides the means to accomplish it. We need not struggle to make it happen. When He wants us to minister to others in whatever way He desires, He will show us exactly what needs to be done. Be free. God's requests are reasonable.

> And God is able to make all grace abound toward you;
> that ye, always having all sufficiency in all things,
> may abound to every good work.
>
> —*2 Corinthians 9:8*

Personal Reflections:

Explain how I seek God's wisdom as to what and where He desires for me to serve Him. How do I obtain the resources needed to accomplish the work He calls me to do?

_____
_____
_____
_____
_____
_____
_____
_____
_____
_____
_____
_____
_____

May 15

We need to consider the lilies. Do they fret about tomorrow? Why should we? We are God's very own children. Our heavenly Father deeply cares for our entire well-being and loves us unconditionally. Anchor your hope in God and in Him alone.

> Now if God so clothes the grass of the field, which today
> is, and tomorrow is thrown into the oven, will He not
> much more clothe you, O you of little faith?
> —*Matthew 6:30 (NKJV)*

Personal Reflections:

Why do I search clothing catalogues to find something to wear? What might happen if I seek God's will and wisdom before shopping?

_____

_____

_____

_____

_____

_____

_____

_____

_____

_____

_____

_____

_____

May 16

Jesus warns us to beware of false leaders within the church. They come disguised as those who appear to be the mature. However, their fruit will reveal whether they are of God or of the world *(1 John 4:1–6)*. The best way to detect a counterfeit is to know the real thing *(2 Timothy 2:15)*.

> Beware of false prophets, which come to you in sheep's clothing, but inwardly they are ravening wolves. Ye shall know them by their fruits. Do men gather grapes of thorns, or figs of thistles?
>
> —*Matthew 7:15–16*

Personal Reflections:

How can I discern who is, and who is not a true prophet even though they may appear to be a mature believer? Describe what sheep's clothing means to me when discerning false prophets, or false teachers.

_____

_____

_____

_____

_____

_____

_____

_____

_____

_____

May 17

The one true God sent Jesus Christ to die for sinful humanity. Jesus willingly laid down His life for everyone *(John 3:16; 4:42)*.

Why does the world look for ways to belittle Jesus' memory and reputation? Why do they care? When people disparage Jesus Christ and His work, even more than two thousand years after His death, this reveals a spiritual truth. A spirit of antichrist is at work *(1 John 2:22; 4:3)*.

If Jesus were a mere man, and not the only begotten Son of God, His memory would have faded long ago. More significantly, He is still the subject of controversy. Jesus is alive! He is coming back for His bride. Get ready *(Revelation 19:7)*.

> The Lord is not slack concerning his promise, as some men count slackness; but is longsuffering to us-ward, not willing that any should perish, but that all should come to repentance.
>
> *—2 Peter 3:9*

Personal Reflections:

Explain what repentance means to me and why I need to search my heart daily. What must I do to be ready when Jesus returns for His bride?

_____

_____

_____

_____

_____

May 18

People who malign or desecrate the work of the cross of Christ and God's only begotten Son condemn themselves. They have chosen to abide in darkness rather than true light *(John 1:8; 3:18)*. Christians need to walk worthy of God and His kingdom, and not allow the tempter to distract them. It is not our job to try to convince others that Jesus Christ is the Son of God.

> And this is the condemnation, that light is come into
> the world, and men loved darkness rather than light,
> because their deeds were evil.
>
> *—John 3:19*

Personal Reflections:

What makes me feel more comfortable, participating in worldly events, or attending church on Sunday? How can I draw closer to God?

_____

_____

_____

_____

_____

_____

_____

_____

_____

_____

_____

Kathe S. Rumsey & Roberta M. Wong

May 19

Do you know what God has purposed for you? Are you following His plans for your life? The disorderly church will continue in ineffective works until each member submits to the headship of Christ in everything, fulfilling the will of God *(Ephesians 5:23; Colossians 1:18)*.

> But as God hath distributed to every man, as the Lord hath called every one, so let him walk. And so ordain I [Paul] in all the churches.
>
> *—1 Corinthians 7:17*

Personal Reflections:

How do I know what God has called me to do? Describe what I believe to be God's plan for my life.

_____

_____

_____

_____

_____

_____

_____

_____

_____

_____

_____

_____

May 20

Many times church members desire to do the work someone else is doing because of prestige, or thinking it will please God. Obedience to God's will is precious in His sight whether called to pastor or wait tables. He does not place a higher value on one over the other. We must understand God has specific plans for each of us to fulfill. Seek His wisdom and do only what He asks of you. He is no respecter of persons; we are all members of the same body *(1 Corinthians 7:18–19).*

> Let each one remain in the same calling in which he was called.
>
> *—1 Corinthians 7:20 (NKJV)*

Personal Reflections:

Have I been faithful to the calling on my life according to God's purpose? How do I resist the temptation to operate in another believer's calling?

Kathe S. Rumsey & Roberta M. Wong

May 21

If we are to follow our Lord and Savior Jesus Christ, we must take up our cross daily and die to our own way of doing things. Just as for the joy set before Him, Jesus endured His cross, we too can endure trials when we focus on the joy set before us *(John 15:11; Hebrews 12:2)*. Rejoice. His joy will be our strength.

> Then he said unto them, Go your way, eat the fat, and drink the sweet, and send portions unto them for whom nothing is prepared: for this day is holy unto our LORD: neither be ye sorry; for the joy of the LORD is your strength.
>
> —*Nehemiah 8:10*

Personal Reflections:

Describe what the joy of the Lord means to me, and its purpose in my life. Describe how difficulties will come to me because I am a follower of Jesus Christ.

_____

_____

_____

_____

_____

_____

_____

_____

_____

May 22

The enormous problems of our world drive many to seek a way of escape. Some surrender their lives to harmful addictions. Others pursue relief by endlessly seeking a better existence in the midst of global decline.

Nevertheless, Christians have a steadfast, Rock-solid hope in Jesus Christ; He is the King of kings. Encourage one another with this good news *(Psalm 11:1–7)*.

> Fearfulness and trembling are come upon me, and horror hath overwhelmed me. And I said, Oh that I had wings like a dove! for then would I fly away, and be at rest.
>
> *—Psalm 55:15*

Personal Reflections:

Describe some of the trials and temptations I have experienced in my life. To whom and where do I turn when trials and temptations challenge me?

_____

_____

_____

_____

_____

_____

_____

_____

_____

Kathe S. Rumsey & Roberta M. Wong

May 23

Jesus Christ is the only begotten Son of God, even our soon coming Bridegroom. It is every Christian's responsibility to get ready *(Matthew 25:1–13; Revelation 19:7).*

> For unto us a child is born, unto us a son is given:
> and the government shall be upon his shoulder: and
> his name shall be called Wonderful, Counselor, The
> mighty God, The everlasting Father, The Prince of
> Peace.
>
> *—Isaiah 9:6*

Personal Reflections:

Explain why Jesus had to die such a horrendous death at Calvary. Explain why it is impossible to find peace without Jesus in my life.

_____

_____

_____

_____

_____

_____

_____

_____

_____

_____

_____

_____

_____

May 24

God asks nothing more from us than to believe in His Son. We can be confident that with Him nothing is impossible *(Mark 10:27)*. Through Christ, God has provided everything for believers and their households to be in a right relationship with their heavenly Father. What God has pledged to do He will do. What awesome news!

> And they said, Believe on the Lord Jesus Christ, and thou shalt be saved, and thy house.
>
> *—Acts 16:31*

Personal Reflections:

What does my belief in the Lord Jesus Christ mean to my household? Explain what God expects from me as a believer.

_____

_____

_____

_____

_____

_____

_____

_____

_____

_____

_____

_____

_____

May 25

What glorious promises of hope we have in Christ the Lord! *(2 Corinthians 1:20).*

> But the mercy of the LORD is from everlasting to everlasting upon them that fear him, and his righteousness unto children's children; to such as keep his covenant, and to those that remember his commandments to do them.
>
> *—Psalm 103:17–18*

Personal Reflections:

Describe ways I might thank the committed believers in my family for living out their witness of Christ Jesus. How has my salvation resulted from hearing the personal testimony of someone else?

_____

_____

_____

_____

_____

_____

_____

_____

_____

_____

_____

_____

_____

_____

May 26

Left to our own abilities, humanity cannot fix the problems it has created. May God grant us mercy and help us return our nation to her godly roots. May He restore and bless America once again as His church humbles herself and prays *(2 Chronicles 7:14)*. In the midst of a world gone mad, may the church proclaim God's glory.

> Turn us back to You, O Lord, and we will be restored;
> renew our days as of old, unless You have utterly
> rejected us, and are very angry with us!
> —*Lamentations 5:21–22 (NKJV)*

Personal Reflections:

How can I apply this verse from Lamentations not only to my life, but also to my prayers? Explain how things turn around when I prioritized prayer and make it the most important part of my day.

_____

_____

_____

_____

_____

_____

_____

_____

_____

_____

_____

_____

Kathe S. Rumsey & Roberta M. Wong

May 27

The church must realize Jesus Christ may return at any moment *(1 Thessalonians 4:16)*. The Book of Revelation exhorts believers to have an ear to hear what the Holy Spirit is saying to the churches. If we lack the fervent love for Jesus Christ we once exhibited, it is time to seek private moments with Him. If we draw near to God, without doubt, He will draw closer to us *(James 4:8)*.

> I know your works, your labor, your patience, and that you cannot bear those who are evil. And you have tested those who say they are apostles and are not, and have found them liars; and you have persevered and have patience, and have labored for My name's sake and have not become weary. Nevertheless I have this against you, that you have left your first love.
>
> *—Revelation 2:2–4 (NKJV)*

Personal Reflections:

How would I feel if God was not pleased with me because of sin? How can I regain the love and spiritual hunger for His presence that I experienced when I was first saved?

_____

_____

_____

_____

_____

_____

_____

May 28

We must hold onto that childlike trust and fervor we first experienced the day Jesus Christ came into our heart and saved us. We must not allow the cares, riches or pleasures of this life to erode our love and confidence in the truth. Now is the time to give the King of glory full reign in our life every day *(Psalm 24:7–8).*

> Take heed, brethren, lest there be in any of you an evil heart of unbelief, in departing from the living God. But exhort one another daily, while it is called Today; lest any of you be hardened through the deceitfulness of sin. For we are made partakers of Christ, if we hold the beginning of our confidence steadfast unto the end; while it is said, Today if ye will hear his voice, harden not your hearts, as in the provocation [rebellion].
>
> *—Hebrews 3:12–15*

Personal Reflections:

How do I exhort others with the truth of God's Word? How can I walk upright in the midst of a rebellious world?

_____

_____

_____

_____

_____

_____

_____

_____

Kathe S. Rumsey & Roberta M. Wong

May 29

If we understand God's commandments regarding life's circumstances, but refuse to obey His Word and trust Him, we will never enter His rest nor share His peace *(John 16:33; Hebrews 3:18–19).*

> Now faith is the substance of things hoped for, the evidence of things not seen.
>
> *—Hebrews 11:1*

Personal Reflections:

What should I do while patiently waiting for God to bring into existence the things I hope for? How can my faith be increased?

_____

_____

_____

_____

_____

_____

_____

_____

_____

_____

_____

_____

_____

_____

_____

May 30

Evil is intensifying *(Psalm 12:8)*. Fraud and immorality attempt to seduce us from every angle. We must resist the allure of idols as well as the excesses of this world. We must be watchful, guarding our heart, and praying always. The end of the age of grace is nearer than when we first believed.

> Now these things were our examples, to the intent we should not lust after evil things, as they also lusted. Neither be ye idolaters, as were some of them; as it is written, The people sat down to eat and drink, and rose up to play. Neither let us commit fornication [sexual immorality], as some of them committed, and fell in one day three and twenty thousand. Now all these things happened unto them for examples: and they are written for our admonition, upon whom the ends of the world [age] are come. Wherefore let him that thinketh he standeth take heed lest he fall.
>
> *—1 Corinthians 10:6–8, 11–12*

Personal Reflections:

Describe how past generations of believers in my family influenced my faith. Explain what I have learned from the Bible concerning the ends of the world [age].

_____

_____

_____

_____

_____

May 31

Temptation is not sin. If we want to overcome, it is our responsibility to take advantage of God's way of escape *(James 1:12)*. God is sovereign. There is not one temptation that comes our way that is not common to all. If we are in Christ, we can resist temptation by arming ourselves with God's Word. When we submit to Him and resist the devil, God will provide a way for us to overcome *(1 Peter 5:8–9)*. He will never allow any of His children to fail. In His merciful kindness, He is longsuffering to bring us to maturity *(2 Peter 3:9)*.

> There hath no temptation taken you but such as is common to man: but God is faithful, who will not suffer [allow] you to be tempted above that ye are able; but will with the temptation also make a way to escape, that ye may be able to bear [endure] it.
>
> *—1 Corinthians 10:13*

Personal Reflections:

How do I recognize temptation when it comes? Describe ways of escape that God has provided in my life.

_____

_____

_____

_____

_____

_____

_____

_____

June 1

Everywhere we go someone has strong convictions concerning what one should eat or not eat. God's Word tells us it is not what goes into our mouth that defiles us but the words that come out of our mouth *(Matthew 15:11)*.

As believers in Jesus Christ, we walk in the liberty He provides *(1 Timothy 4:3–5)*. We must not be deceived; the enemy will use this liberty to sow divisions among us. Do not allow the idols of others to undermine your work for the Lord.

> If any of them that believe not bid you to a feast, and ye be disposed to go; whatsoever is set before you, eat, asking no question for conscience sake. But if any man say unto you, This is offered in sacrifice unto idols, eat not for his sake that showed it, and for conscience sake: for the earth is the Lord's, and the fullness thereof.
>
> *—1 Corinthians 10:27–28*

Personal Reflections:

Explain the liberty I walk in as a genuine follower of Christ. Jesus dined and fellowshipped with anyone who invited Him; how do I respond to the doors He opens for me?

_____

_____

_____

_____

_____

_____

Kathe S. Rumsey & Roberta M. Wong

June 2

The world continues to defy God's order. The baby-boom generation can remember when the institution of marriage came under grave attack; the roles of the husband and the wife were denigrated. In defiance to the Word of God, society urged wives to assert their own identity and answer to no one. They were manipulated into believing they do not have to submit to their husbands as head *(Ephesians 5:23)*. Many did not realize this idea originated from a spirit of rebellion. Through his clever lies, Satan still attempts to deceive and destroy mankind. The truth is that God provided the husband as a spiritual cover for the wife, just as Christ is to the church, the savior of His body.

> But I would have you know, that the head of every man
> is Christ; and the head of woman is the man; and the
> head of Christ is God.
>   —*1 Corinthians 11:3*

Personal Reflections:

When did division in the marriage originate? Explain my willingness to accept Christ as the head of the church, just as the husband is the head of the wife.

_____

_____

_____

_____

_____

_____

_____

June 3

Scripture equates the relationship of husband and wife to Christ and His church. Far too few men and women have lasting marriage relationships because of a lack of commitment in their relationship with Christ first. Scripture states that God ordained marriage between a man and a woman. The truth is marriage unites the two into one flesh *(Mark 10:6–8)*.

> For the husband is the head of the wife, even as Christ is the head of the church: and he is the savior of the body.
>
> *—Ephesians 5:23*

Personal Reflections:

Describe what it means to me to submit to my own husband in everything. Explain God's justification for my submitting to my own husband according to His Word.

_____

_____

_____

_____

_____

_____

_____

_____

_____

_____

_____

_____

June 4

The body of Christ is only as healthy as its weakest member. Compromise with the world and denominationalism divide and diminish the authority and power of Jesus' church *(Ephesians 4:3)*. There is one body, one Spirit, one hope, one Lord, one faith, one baptism, one God and Father of all *(Ephesians 4:4–6)*. Be faithful to minister Christ's love to one another as the Day draws near.

> For God is not unrighteous to forget your work and labor of love, which ye have showed toward his name, in that ye have ministered to the saints, and do minister. And we desire that every one of you do show the same diligence to the full assurance of hope unto the end.
>
> *—Hebrews 6:10–11*

Personal Reflections:

What is my role is in the body of Christ? Describe how I can faithfully fulfill my part in God's plan.

_____

_____

_____

_____

_____

_____

_____

_____

June 5

No, not one of us can claim to be sinless *(Romans 3:23)*. Our world, just like the Titanic, has benefited from man's finest engineering, wealth, and opulence. Yet we live in a world where, in one fleeting moment, it can all become a death trap when the pride of man is at the helm.

> And it came to pass, as Jesus sat at meat in the house, behold, many publicans and sinners came and sat down with him and his disciples. And when the Pharisees saw it, they said unto his disciples, Why eateth your Master with publicans and sinners? But when Jesus heard that, he said unto them, They that be whole need not a physician, but they that are sick. But go ye and learn what that meaneth, I will have mercy, and not sacrifice: for I am not come to call the righteous, but sinners to repentance.
>
> *—Matthew 9:10–13*

Personal Reflections:

Explain my willingness to do as Jesus did, sitting down and dining with sinners and publicans. What does repentance mean to me, and have I turned from my own sin?

_____

_____

_____

_____

_____

_____

Kathe S. Rumsey & Roberta M. Wong

June 6

It is God's will that not one person should perish but that all would have a change of heart and repent *(2 Peter 3:9)*. God is longsuffering. He patiently works in us, building His children into the fullness of Christ *(Ephesians 4:13)*. How much more emphatic can the Word of God be that Jesus Christ is the God of salvation for the whole world!

> This is a faithful saying, and worthy of all acceptation, that Christ Jesus came into the world to save sinners; of whom I [Paul] am chief. Howbeit for this cause I obtained mercy, that in me first Jesus Christ might show forth all longsuffering, for a pattern to them which should hereafter believe on him to life everlasting.
>
> *—1 Timothy 1:15–16*

Personal Reflections:

Explain how I can demonstrate to others the same patience God has shown toward me. Explain how I can genuinely show compassion toward others knowing God desires none should perish.

_____

_____

_____

_____

_____

_____

_____

June 7

God's Word tells us how we are to respond to men and women appointed to positions of authority. When we are tempted to criticize others in leadership, the Word of God instructs us to pray and intercede for these individuals *(Ephesians 6:12)*. Encourage others who may be concerned and exhort them to pray also, so we may experience a godly and peaceable life.

> I [Paul] exhort therefore, that, first of all, supplications, prayers, intercessions, and giving of thanks, be made for all men; for kings, and for all that are in authority; that we may lead a quiet and peaceable life in all godliness and honesty. For this is good and acceptable in the sight of God our Savior; who will have all men to be saved, and to come unto the knowledge of the truth. For there is one God, and one mediator between God and men, the man Christ Jesus: who gave himself a ransom for all, to be testified in due time.
>
> *—1 Timothy 2:1–6*

Personal Reflections:

Explain why I am willing to pray for all who are in authority. What is my part in assuring that we lead a quiet and peaceable life?

_____

_____

_____

_____

_____

_____

Kathe S. Rumsey & Roberta M. Wong

June 8

Spiritually, the husband is the wife's protective covering; he is her God-ordained head. If a wife submits to her own husband even though circumstances appear unfavorable, God's protective cover remains *(Ephesians 5:22)*. When God's order of authority rules, the gates of hell cannot prevail against the church.

> Let the woman learn in silence with all subjection. But I suffer not a woman to teach, nor to usurp authority over the man, but to be in silence. For Adam was first formed, and then Eve. And Adam was not deceived, but the woman being deceived was in the transgression.
>
> *—1 Timothy 2:11–14*

Personal Reflections:

Explain how I came to understand why the Creator of the universe made the woman to be in subjection to the man. What, if anything, bothers me concerning the role of the wife submitting to the headship of her own husband?

_____

_____

_____

_____

_____

_____

_____

_____

_____

June 9

God commands the church to honor its widows. His Word tells us it is the responsibility of children to respect and value their parents. Even though we live in a mobile society, this does not negate the duty we have to our parents, especially widowed mothers. When we fulfill our obligations, this frees the church to fulfill their biblical responsibility to care for true widows needing assistance.

> Honor widows that are widows indeed. But if any widow have children or nephews, let them learn first to show piety at home, and to requite [repay] their parents: for that is good and acceptable before God
>
> —*1 Timothy 5:3–4*

Personal Reflections:

Who might be a widow in my church without family members living in her vicinity? What widow in my church has absolutely no one to check in on her well-being?

_____

_____

_____

_____

_____

_____

_____

_____

_____

_____

Kathe S. Rumsey & Roberta M. Wong

June 10

Do you know someone in your church or in your neighborhood who is a true widow? How might you make a difference in her life? Just as God stipulates responsibility to honor widows, reciprocally, widows are encouraged to trust Him and to continue in supplications and prayers.

> Now she that is a widow indeed, and desolate, trusteth in God, and continueth in supplications and prayers night and day.
>
> —*1 Timothy 5:5*

Personal Reflections:

How might I seek God's will to see if I should organize a group for the widows in my church? In what way has He prepared me to lead a widow's group in fervent prayer for one another's needs?

_____

_____

_____

_____

_____

_____

_____

_____

_____

_____

_____

_____

June 11

In a world frivolously attempting to amuse itself with nonessentials, God's wisdom is necessary to prioritize our time and resources to assist those who genuinely have a need. Help may not always be financial; sometimes it could be to alleviate loneliness; others may just need someone to listen.

> But if any provide not for his own, and especially for those of his own house, he hath denied the faith, and is worse than an infidel [unbeliever].
>
> —*1 Timothy 5:8*

Personal Reflections:

Has God given me the ability to identify the needs of widows, and how to meet those needs? Have I received a rhema word from the Holy Spirit concerning a specific widow's need?

_____

_____

_____

_____

_____

_____

_____

_____

_____

_____

_____

_____

Kathe S. Rumsey & Roberta M. Wong

June 12

As Christians, we must be doers of the Word, not hearers only. Caring for the widows in our own households will free the church to assist those who truly have no family to help them. Offering our assistance to widows without being asked could be a great blessing.

> If any believing man or woman has widows, let them relieve them, and do not let the church be burdened, that it may relieve those who are really widows.
> —*1 Timothy 5:16 (NKJV)*

Personal Reflections:

Who are the widows in my family? Explain how I could be of assistance to my grandmother, mother, aunt, or even an aging sister.

_____

_____

_____

_____

_____

_____

_____

_____

_____

_____

_____

June 13

Because many false prophets and teachers infiltrate the church, Scripture warns us to guard our hearts *(Proverbs 4:23)*. The forces of deceptive words easily seduce us into destructive ways. When God's truth is perverted, many are too easily misled. Do not be deceived. Test the spirits *(1 John 4:1–6)*.

> But there were false prophets also among the people, even as there shall be false teachers among you, who privily shall bring in damnable [destructive] heresies, even denying the Lord that bought them, and bring upon themselves swift destruction. And many shall follow their pernicious ways; by reason of whom the way of truth shall be evil spoken of. And through covetousness shall they with feigned words make merchandise of you: whose judgment now of a long time lingereth not, and their damnation slumbereth not.
>
> *—2 Peter 2:1–3*

Personal Reflections:

With many versions of the Bible available, describe what I need for my personal study of God's Word. Explain how I might benefit from the use of a concordance to research Scripture verses.

_____

_____

_____

_____

_____

_____

Kathe S. Rumsey & Roberta M. Wong

June 14

Believers will identify false prophets and false teachers by their fruit. Do not be deceived; they are self-serving *(Matthew 7:15–20)*. Jesus reminds us that no one can serve God and mammon *(Matthew 6:24)*.

> But these speak evil of those things which they know
> not: but what they know naturally, as brute beasts, in
> those things they corrupt themselves. Woe unto them!
> for they have gone in the way of Cain, and ran greedily
> after the error of Balaam for reward, and perished in
> the gainsaying of Core.
>
> *—Jude vs. 10–11*

Personal Reflections:

Describe how the Word of God is my only source of genuine truth in a world filled with lies and deception. When I hear people speak evil of God's Word how does it make me feel?

_____

_____

_____

_____

_____

_____

_____

_____

_____

_____

_____

June 15

Jesus tells us that those that follow Him are salt and light *(Matthew 5:13–16)*. We are in the world, but not of it. We are not to pander to the world's values to avoid confrontation and persecution. As the children of God, we must utilize the whole armor of God and speak the truth in love. This is not the hour for compromise. Therefore, pray in the Spirit on all occasions *(Ephesians 6:18-20)*. God will equip us with the boldness we need to speak His truth in love.

> But, beloved, remember ye the words which were spoken before of the apostles of our Lord Jesus Christ; how that they told you there should be mockers in the last time, who should walk after their own ungodly lusts. These be they who separate themselves, sensual, having not the Spirit. But ye, beloved, building up yourselves on your most holy faith, praying in the Holy Ghost, keep yourselves in the love of God, looking for the mercy of our Lord Jesus Christ unto eternal life.
>
> *—Jude vs. 17–21*

Personal Reflections:

Explain how praying in the Holy Spirit builds my faith. How can I keep myself in the love of God, seeking His mercy, looking for Christ's return?

_____

_____

_____

_____

_____

Kathe S. Rumsey & Roberta M. Wong

June 16

Peter, the apostle, forewarns the church that fiery trials will test our faith; we will suffer for the Word's sake. Even when we may feel we cannot endure another moment, we must stand on the promises of God *(Galatians 6:9)*. God is faithful to His Word regarding our past, present, and future *(1 Peter 1:5–9)*. The joy of the Lord is our strength *(Nehemiah 8:10)*.

> But the God of all grace, who hath called us unto His eternal glory by Christ Jesus, after that ye have suffered a while, make you perfect, establish, strengthen, settle you.
>
> *—1 Peter 5:10*

Personal Reflections:

Explain how a loving God might allow bad things to happen to me for a good reason. Why does it seem like things get tougher the longer I follow Christ Jesus?

_____

_____

_____

_____

_____

_____

_____

_____

_____

_____

June 17

The Word of God is a resourceful storehouse of God's provision that enables true success and enriches our lives. If we diligently seek God's will in everything we say and do, He promises to supply us with the wisdom we need to succeed in every area. Only Jesus Christ is the way to God the Father *(John 14:6)*.

> This book of the law shall not depart out of thy mouth;
> but thou shalt meditate therein day and night, that thou
> mayest observe to do according to all that is written
> therein: for then thou shalt make thy way prosperous,
> and then thou shalt have good success.
>
> *—Joshua 1:8*

Personal Reflections:

Explain why I honestly believe the Bible is the best training manual for my life. Explain how the Bible is still relevant for my success in this generation even though it has been around for centuries.

_____

_____

_____

_____

_____

_____

_____

_____

_____

_____

Kathe S. Rumsey & Roberta M. Wong

June 18

Daily, the world strives to manipulate and bombard us with falsehoods *(John 8:43–44)*. If we are ever to carry out the will of God as His sons and daughters, we must renew our mind with the Word of God *(Romans 12:2)*. Our transformation begins the moment we live by faith in the Son of God, and obey Him.

> I beseech you therefore, brethren, by the mercies of God, that ye present your bodies a living sacrifice, holy, acceptable to God, which is your reasonable service.
>
> *—Romans 12:1*

Personal Reflections:

How can I present my body as a living sacrifice, my reasonable service? Why should I invest my time building my faith?

_____

_____

_____

_____

_____

_____

_____

_____

_____

_____

_____

June 19

Jesus paid a high price for our salvation, emptying Himself completely for our sake. His precious and priceless blood redeemed us from the curse of the law *(Galatians 3:13–14)*. Walk in this truth! Walk boldly, knowing that you are a child of the most high God.

> For I [John] rejoiced greatly, when the brethren came
> and testified of the truth that is in thee, even as thou
> walkest in the truth.
>
> *—3 John vs. 3*

Personal Reflections:

Explain how I walk in the truth of the good news of Christ Jesus. Describe how I seek to know Jesus more and more each day.

_____

_____

_____

_____

_____

_____

_____

_____

_____

_____

_____

_____

_____

_____

June 20

Jesus has kept the promise of His Word to us; we are not alone. The Holy Spirit is available to every born-again child of God. Not only is He our Comforter in this world, He is our teacher, advocate, and companion who guides us into all truth. Thanks be to our Lord and Savior Jesus Christ for this wonderful gift.

> And I will pray the Father, and he shall give you another Comforter, that he may abide with you forever; even the Spirit of truth; whom the world cannot receive, because it seeth him not, neither knoweth him: but ye know him; for he dwelleth with you, and shall be in you.
>
> *—John 14:16–17*

Personal Reflections:

How can I receive the Spirit of truth into my life? Describe times when I feel alone in this world and how I reach out to God through His Holy Spirit to bring me comfort.

_____

_____

_____

_____

_____

_____

_____

_____

_____

June 21

No matter how intense our challenges and obstacles of faith become in this present-day's world, God remains faithful. His Word encourages us with hope and brings light into every situation. All things do work together for our good. Fear not. God has given us a spirit of power, love, and a disciplined mind *(2 Timothy 1:7)*. Do not allow the cares of this life to distract you. Focus on the One who deserves our love and obedience. He alone is faithful.

> And we know that all things work together for good to them that love God, to them who are the called according to his purpose.
>
> *—Romans 8:28*

Personal Reflections:

How do I let go and trust God to work everything for my good even when the world is crumbling down around me? Explain why I am confident I have been called according to His purpose.

_____

_____

_____

_____

_____

_____

_____

_____

_____

_____

June 22

The Holy Spirit of God, whom Jesus promised to send to us, will teach us all things. Do not be deceived by those who serve themselves and the world. Jesus said the mature of the flock know His voice; they follow Him and not hirelings *(John 10:12, 27)*.

> These things have I written unto you concerning them that seduce you. But the anointing which ye have received of him abideth in you, and ye need not that any man teach you: but as the same anointing teacheth you of all things, and is truth, and is no lie, and even as it hath taught you, ye shall abide in him.
>
> *—1 John 2:26–27*

Personal Reflections:

Explain why I trust the Holy Spirit, as my teacher, to lead me into all truth. How can I recognize God's truth, and avoid listening to those who preach doctrines contrary to His Word?

_____

_____

_____

_____

_____

_____

_____

_____

_____

_____

June 23

It is now the 23rd day of June. Almost half a year has passed before us. Let us pause and ask ourselves if we have redeemed our time wisely for the kingdom of God in obedience to His will. We know if we ask God for wisdom, He will provide it abundantly *(James 1:5)*. Each remaining day still offers a new opportunity to serve God Almighty and prepare for Christ's return. What higher calling could there be? *(Philippians 3:13–14)*.

> So teach us to number our days, that we may apply our hearts unto wisdom.
>
> *—Psalm 90:12*

Personal Reflections:

How can I redeem the time in which I live? Describe how I seek God's wisdom to solve the problems of my life, and those of the world.

_____

_____

_____

_____

_____

_____

_____

_____

_____

_____

_____

Kathe S. Rumsey & Roberta M. Wong

June 24

Apostle Paul's warnings to Timothy hold true nowadays. What some falsely call knowledge regarding the truth of the gospel of God in fact contradicts the doctrine of Christ *(1 Timothy 6:3–5)*. Many have strayed concerning the faith; apostasy is on the rise. God have mercy on us. Difficult is the way that leads to eternal life. Only truth keeps our feet firmly planted on the narrow path of life *(Matthew 7:14)*.

> O Timothy, keep that which is committed to thy trust, avoiding profane and vain babblings, and oppositions of science [knowledge] falsely so called: which some professing have erred concerning the faith. Grace be with thee. Amen.
>
> *—1 Timothy 6:20–21*

Personal Reflections:

How many mature Christians do I know personally? Explain why I spend time with committed believers rightly dividing the Word of God.

_____

_____

_____

_____

_____

_____

_____

_____

_____

June 25

It is time to clean house. As Christians, we must safeguard how we occupy our time, what we allow ourselves to see and hear. The little things in our lives that seem insignificant can be the most damaging. The seeds of the enemy will produce a crop of deception *(Galatians 5:7–9)*. How many times have we viewed a movie or television program only to fast forward or mute it to avoid unacceptable images and words?

Worldly media does not endorse the truth of God's Word. Why do we spend our time and money on ungodly things that have no value? Compromise in little things misleads us into deception.

> For many deceivers have gone out into the world who do not confess Jesus Christ as coming in the flesh. This is a deceiver and an antichrist. If anyone comes to you and does not bring this doctrine, do not receive him into your house nor greet him.
>
> *—2 John vs. 7, 10 (NKJV)*

Personal Reflections:

How will I recognize the antichrist spirits operating in the world? There are many people who speak eloquently, yet falsely, concerning God's Word. How can I distinguish the genuine?

_____
_____
_____
_____
_____
_____

Kathe S. Rumsey & Roberta M. Wong

June 26

Currently our culture equates those standing for God's principles as being naïve and narrow-minded. Numerous Christians follow articulate individuals who spout worldly wisdom; deceptive words and flattery mislead many *(2 Peter 2:1–3)*.

Present day Christians live in an environment in which, if possible, even the elect could be deceived *(Matthew 24:24)*. Believers must pray, seek God and His wisdom in this hour. Hear what the Holy Spirit is saying to you personally and then do it *(Revelation 3:22)*.

> Now I [Paul] beseech you, brethren, mark them which cause divisions and offenses contrary to the doctrine which ye have learned; and avoid them. For they that are such serve not our Lord Jesus Christ, but their own belly [emotions]; and by good words and fair speeches deceive the hearts of the simple
>
> *—Romans 16:17–18*

Personal Reflections:

Explain how I evaluate Christ's doctrine: based upon the Word of God, or on denominational teaching. Would I be willing to leave a church led by a pastor who allows division and offenses to control the congregation?

_____

_____

_____

_____

_____

June 27

The only source of true comfort comes from God's presence as we read Scripture and allow the Holy Spirit of God to instruct us *(Philippians 2:2; 1 John 1:3).*

> For whatsoever things were written aforetime were written for our learning, that we through patience and comfort of the Scriptures might have hope.
>
> *—Romans 15:4*

Personal Reflections:

Explain how I have completely put my faith in God and His Word. Explain how the Holy Spirit as my Comforter and teacher leads me into all truth.

_____
_____
_____
_____
_____
_____
_____
_____
_____
_____
_____
_____
_____
_____
_____

June 28

Never take the gift of faith for granted. Are we confident in the gospel of Jesus Christ? If persecuted for our beliefs, will our faith stand? In His love, share the truth of God's salvation message as His Spirit leads. Redeem the time.

> For I long to see you, that I may impart unto you some spiritual gift, to the end ye may be established; that is, that I may be comforted together with you by the mutual faith both of you and me.
>
> —*Romans 1:11–12*

Personal Reflections:

Describe how I can comfort others in need because I am secure in my faith. Why do I prefer to fellowship with other believers who are Rock-solid in their faith and know to stand in agreement?

_____

_____

_____

_____

_____

_____

_____

_____

_____

_____

_____

_____

June 29

In this hour of deception, the body of Christ needs one another in order to stand strong. We need to stay connected *(Hebrews 10:24–25)*. For many of us, it is difficult to reach out to others. However, if we view one another as members of God's family, it becomes easier to introduce ourselves and extend our hand of assistance.

As the pressures of persecution increase, Satan's forces diminish when believers assemble in faith *(Matthew 18:19–20)*. We must not allow the difficulties and distractions of this world to deter us from prayer and Bible study.

> Wherefore be ye not unwise, but understanding what the will of the Lord is. And be not drunk with wine, wherein is excess; but be filled with the Spirit; speaking to yourselves in psalms and hymns and spiritual songs, singing and making melody in your heart to the Lord.
>
> —*Ephesians 5:17–19*

Personal Reflections:

Explain how I can truly understand the will of God in every situation. Explain how turning to psalms, hymns, and spiritual songs to fill my heart with praise to God restores my soul.

_____

_____

_____

_____

_____

_____

Kathe S. Rumsey & Roberta M. Wong

June 30

Jesus Christ is the King of kings, the Lord of lords. The Father and His Son Jesus Christ are one *(John 17:11)*. When we, God's children, see ourselves as our heavenly Father sees us, unconditional love toward others becomes second nature. Reach out to someone who may seem unlovely, even hostile, making a difference in his or her life. As God's children, we represent our heavenly Father to others here on earth.

> Be ye therefore followers of God as dear children: and
> walk in love, as Christ also hath loved us, and hath
> given himself for us an offering and a sacrifice to God
> for a sweetsmelling savor.
> *—Ephesians 5:1–2*

Personal Reflections:

How do I make time to walk in love as a child of God? Describe how others might experience God's love through my witness.

_____

_____

_____

_____

_____

_____

_____

_____

_____

_____

July 1

Sin is sin. Criticism and love are incompatible. As children of God, we are to put Jesus' commandment of love into action, and not be swayed by the world's behavior *(Ephesians 5:1–5)*. God has generously forgiven us, and we are to forgive others in the same manner. Our merciful Father's love toward all is unconditional. We must walk in the same love toward others that He extends to us.

> Be ye therefore merciful, as your Father also is merciful. Judge not, and ye shall not be judged: condemn not, and ye shall not be condemned: forgive, and ye shall be forgiven.
>
> *—Luke 6:36–37*

Personal Reflections:

Why do I judge others based upon worldly wisdom? Would it make a difference if I view others through the perspective of my heavenly Father?

_____

_____

_____

_____

_____

_____

_____

_____

_____

_____

Kathe S. Rumsey & Roberta M. Wong

July 2

Any day, Jesus Christ can return for His bride; that should be the focus of His church. A bride, who prepares herself for her future role, focuses on the one she loves with all her heart. Worldly temptations cannot distract her. If our hearts are truly fixed on Jesus Christ, we will be ready for whatever comes our way. The Bridegroom is coming. Go out to meet Him *(Matthew 25:6).*

> For yourselves know perfectly that the day of the Lord
> so cometh as a thief in the night.
>
> *—1 Thessalonians 5:2*

Personal Reflections:

What must I do differently to be ready when Jesus returns? *(Revelation 19:7).* Describe what it means to come as a thief in the night.

_____

_____

_____

_____

_____

_____

_____

_____

_____

_____

_____

_____

_____

July 3

We know crime and immorality abound in present-day society. Reports of evil bombard us daily. *Matthew 25:1–13* tells us half who profess to know Jesus Christ will not be ready when He returns for His bride. It is time to utilize each day wisely to build upon God's truth in preparation for Jesus' return *(1 Thessalonians 4:15–17; Revelation 19:7)*.

> The coming of the lawless one is according to the working of Satan, with all power, signs, and lying wonders, and with all unrighteous deception among those who perish, because they did not receive the love of the truth, that they might be saved.
>
> —*2 Thessalonians 2:9–10 (NKJV)*

Personal Reflections:

What will take place when the lawless one, the son of perdition is revealed? If I am not ready for Jesus' return, what will I need to do to survive the son of perdition's reign on earth?

_____

_____

_____

_____

_____

_____

_____

_____

_____

_____

Kathe S. Rumsey & Roberta M. Wong

July 4

Society's declarations have gone too far and have led generations down a path of moral devastation. Godly wisdom demands we stop flaunting immorality. The church needs to be a moral compass for its members, our nation, and the world. Pray like your life depends upon it while the opportunity still exists *(2 Chronicles 7:14; Matthew 21:13)*. Only God can restore our nation to her godly foundation.

> The wicked walk on every side, when the vilest men are exalted.
> —*Psalm 12:8*

> See then that ye walk circumspectly, not as fools, but as wise, redeeming the time, because the days are evil.
> —*Ephesians 5:15–16*

Personal Reflections:

Explain how I know the wicked are walking in the open. What must I do to redeem the time in which I live?

_____

_____

_____

_____

_____

_____

_____

_____

July 5

Not all the wealth amassed in one's lifetime compensates for even one life missing eternity. Riches of this world are temporary. The salvation of God is eternal.

> Be thou diligent to know the state of thy flocks, and look well [attend] to thy herds. For riches are not forever: and doth the crown endure to every generation?
>
> —*Proverbs 27:23–24*

Personal Reflections:

God's Word exhorts me to feed His sheep; what does that mean? Describe how I have been faithful and obedient to God and His Word.

_____

_____

_____

_____

_____

_____

_____

_____

_____

_____

_____

_____

_____

Kathe S. Rumsey & Roberta M. Wong

July 6

True love does not support anything that may destroy an individual's life and jeopardize their future. Just because society sanctions all manner of sin, the Bible clarifies any questions we may have concerning God's truth *(1 Corinthians 6:9–11)*. God have mercy on us before it is too late.

> The wicked flee when no man pursues, but the righteous are bold as a lion. Because of the transgression of a land many are its princes; but by a man of understanding and knowledge right will be prolonged.
>
> *—Proverbs 28:1–2 (NKJV)*

Personal Reflections:

When Christ returns, will He find me bold as a lion and obeying His commandments? When the wicked are closing in all around, how do I maintain boldness and courage?

_____

_____

_____

_____

_____

_____

_____

_____

_____

_____

_____

_____

July 7

In a true Republic, voting is a privilege. Extreme forethought is necessary to exercise that liberty. Before we mark our ballots, we must pray and seek God's direction *(Proverbs 3:5–7)*. Even if it appears too late to have godly men and women in authority, we are not without hope *(1 Timothy 2:1–3)*. Only God can restore what is broken.

> When the righteous are in authority, the people rejoice:
> but when a wicked beareth rule, the people mourn.
>
> *—Proverbs 29:2*

Personal Reflections:

Whether someone is my choice or not, how do I react when God puts them into a position of authority? Describe what it means for me to have ears to hear what the Holy Spirit is saying to the churches.

_____

_____

_____

_____

_____

_____

_____

_____

_____

_____

_____

Kathe S. Rumsey & Roberta M. Wong

July 8

When the 9/11 attack occurred on American soil, the people of our nation filled churches. Sadly, as the shock of the tragedy subsided, the need for God diminished.

Then again, when hurricane Katrina ripped the southern border of the United States, God became prominent on our lips for a brief moment. If God is love, why approach Him only when disaster strikes? Come to know Him because He desires to love you as a father loves his children. Do not waste another moment. Repent and return to Him *(James 4:8)*.

> If thou wilt return, O Israel, sayeth the LORD, return
> unto me: and if thou wilt put away thine abominations
> out of my sight, then shalt thou not remove [be moved].
> And thou shalt swear, The LORD liveth, in truth, in
> judgment, and in righteousness; and the nations shall
> bless themselves in him, and in him shall they glory.
> —*Jeremiah 4:1–2*

Personal Reflections:

Describe ways in which I may have become distant from God. Explains what takes place if I draw near to God.

_____

_____

_____

_____

_____

_____

_____

July 9

The seductive hypocrisy of politicians blinds the minds of those willing to compromise God's principles. Vile perversion has taken us down a path where God is no longer revered, nor worshipped as our Creator *(Galatians 6:7–8)*. Church, wake up!

> Surely as a wife treacherously departeth from her husband, so have ye dealt treacherously with me, O house of Israel, saith the LORD. A voice was heard upon the high places, weeping and supplications of the children of Israel: for they have perverted their way, and they have forgotten the LORD their God.
>
> *—Jeremiah 3:20–21*

Personal Reflections:

In what ways have I departed from the Living God? What must I do to reject the presence of compromise in my life?

_____

_____

_____

_____

_____

_____

_____

_____

_____

_____

_____

Kathe S. Rumsey & Roberta M. Wong

July 10

The God of our salvation, Jesus Christ, is the same yesterday, today and forever *(Hebrews 13:8)*. He loves us unconditionally. If our walk with God has not been consistent, we must repent *(James 4:8–10)*. He is the only One who possesses the power and authority to save us, America, and our world.

> Let the heaven and earth praise him [LORD], the seas, and every thing that moveth therein. For God will save Zion, and will build the cities of Judah: that they may dwell there, and have it in possession. The seed also of his servants shall inherit it: and they that love his name shall dwell therein.
>
> *—Psalm 69:34–36*

Personal Reflections:

What provision has God made for my family? Describe how my life is a witness of His love and faithfulness to others?

_____

_____

_____

_____

_____

_____

_____

_____

_____

_____

_____

July 11

When the luxuries and delicacies of the world tempt us, remember it is only in God and His provisions that we have true satisfaction. Our inheritance in the kingdom of God far exceeds the fleeting contentment the world offers. Unconditional love and the joy of God's presence in our lives testify to the world around us.

> But Daniel purposed in his heart that he would not defile himself with the portion of the king's meat [delicacies], nor with the wine which he drank: therefore he requested of the prince of the eunuchs that he might not defile himself.
>
> —*Daniel 1:8*

Personal Reflections:

How do I respond to a worldly invitation? Explain how God will move on my behalf if I make the appropriate choices according to His Word.

_____

_____

_____

_____

_____

_____

_____

_____

_____

_____

July 12

If we truly believe the Lord's arrival is forthcoming, our actions will support our words. Preparing our homes to meet any emergency in order to aid others in crises is prudent. Though it may cost them their life, some will accept Jesus Christ as Lord and Savior during the tribulation period *(Revelation 20:4).*

> What doth it profit, my brethren, though a man say he hath faith, and have not works? can faith save him? If a brother or sister be naked, and destitute of daily food, and one of you says unto them, Depart in peace, be ye warmed and filled; notwithstanding ye give them not those things which are needful to the body; what doth it profit? Even so faith, if it hath not works, is dead, being alone.
>
> *—James 2:14–17*

Personal Reflections:

How do I respond when someone has a need? Describe how I can put my faith into action with the leading of the Holy Spirit, and meet the needs of others.

_____

_____

_____

_____

_____

_____

_____

July 13

In obedience to Christ, we must examine ourselves and consider if we have withheld anything from God. Is it our time, talents, money, or stamina? Satan tempts us to put our interest first. Then, if anything is left, we can give that to God. In other words, we can give God our leftovers, or seconds after we have taken care of ourselves. In truth, when we honor God by putting Him first, He provides all our needs.

> But Peter said, Ananias, why hath Satan filled thine heart to lie to the Holy Ghost, and to keep back part of the price of the land? whiles it remained, was it not thine own? and after it was sold, was it not in thine own power? why hast thou conceived this thing in thine heart? thou hast not lied unto men, but unto God.
>
> —*Acts 5:3–4*

Personal Reflections:

Have I ever been tempted to hold back a pledge from God? Explain what I must do when the enemy tempts me to cheat God out of something that already belongs to Him.

_____

_____

_____

_____

_____

_____

_____

_____

Kathe S. Rumsey & Roberta M. Wong

July 14

People who habitually practice evil have already rejected the light. Christians do not need to entice the world into the four walls of our churches to have them accept Jesus Christ as their Lord and Savior. When churches duplicate worldly systems and programs to draw people into their congregations, this is hypocrisy. Please God, deliver us from such a perverted religious mentality.

When someone comes to a congregation on their own free will, we will know God the Father has drawn them to the light, Jesus Christ *(John 6:44)*.

> For every one that doeth evil hateth the light, neither cometh to the light, lest his deeds should be reproved.
> —*John 3:20*

Personal Reflections:

How do I respond to those who hate the light? Explain what I would do if an unbeliever shows up at church by themselves.

_____

_____

_____

_____

_____

_____

_____

_____

_____

_____

July 15

Everyone recognizes that the world is becoming darker, and darker, and darker. One only has to hear the voices of the daily news to know that mankind has lost all sense of decency and morality. As believers of the gospel of God, we will walk in the light when we follow Jesus Christ. Where is He leading you? Follow Him; He is the only way *(John 14:6)*.

> Then spake Jesus again unto them, saying, I am the
> light of the world: he that followeth me shall not walk
> in darkness, but shall have the light of life.
>
> *—John 8:12*

Personal Reflections:

Describe how I feel when confused by the options of the world, and the options of the church for my life. Things are getting darker and darker in the world; how should I respond?

_____

_____

_____

_____

_____

_____

_____

_____

_____

_____

_____

July 16

When will we realize this temporary world offers us nothing in comparison to what God has generously planned for us, now and forever? We are His very own children, whom He loves unconditionally. How can we cheapen ourselves by allowing friendship with the world to take precedence over our relationship with our heavenly Father, God Almighty?

> Ye adulterers and adulteresses, know ye not that the friendship of the world is enmity with God? whosoever therefore will be a friend of the world is the enemy of God.
>
> —*James 4:4*

Personal Reflections:

Would I describe myself a believer, or an enemy of God? Describe how I spend my time: in companionship with God, or with those of the world.

_____

_____

_____

_____

_____

_____

_____

_____

_____

_____

July 17

If we do not allow the Holy Spirit of God to shepherd us through His Word, we will miss true peace in the hurried chaos of daily living. Only He can provide the rest, peace, and fulfillment needed to restore our souls (mind, will, emotions).

> The LORD is my shepherd; I shall not want. He maketh me to lie down in green pastures: he leadeth me beside the still waters. He restoreth my soul: he leadeth me in the paths of righteousness for his name's sake.
>
> *—Psalm 23:1–3*

Personal Reflections:

Describe what being at peace means to me. Explain the difference between following the leading of the Holy Spirit in all I do, or seeking to do things my own way.

_____

_____

_____

_____

_____

_____

_____

_____

_____

_____

_____

Kathe S. Rumsey & Roberta M. Wong

July 18

The Lord Jesus Christ's life is a godly example of a life well-pleasing to God. How did He spend His time? What was important to Him? We must learn to view our life from God's perspective just as Jesus did. Whatever this moment brings, we can follow the Lord's example to live our life to its fullest.

> I [Paul] know both how to be abased, and I know how to abound: every where and in all things I am instructed both to be full and to be hungry, both to abound and to suffer need. I can do all things through Christ which strengtheneth me.
>
> —*Philippians 4:12–13*

Personal Reflections:

Would I be better off if I plan my life according to my own interest and desires, or according to the will of God for me? How do I react when things do not go my way?

_____

_____

_____

_____

_____

_____

_____

_____

_____

_____

July 19

Through the shed blood of Jesus Christ, God has delivered us from sin's bondage and death *Colossians 1:14)*. How do we show Him our gratitude for our redemption? Do we occupy our lives with idols and other gods? We must reject the enticement of this world's frivolities *(1 John 5:21)*.

> I am the LORD thy God, which brought thee out of the land of Egypt, from the house of bondage. Thou shalt have none other gods before me.
>
> —Deuteronomy 5:6–7

Personal Reflections:

Out of ignorance, have I fallen into bondage serving other gods? How can I recognize the One true God?

_____

_____

_____

_____

_____

_____

_____

_____

_____

_____

_____

_____

_____

Kathe S. Rumsey & Roberta M. Wong

July 20

As Christians, we are neither to create nor cater to false gods or idols. We must worship and serve the one true God, not His creation. Only God is to receive our full adoration. Our choices will reap future consequences upon our children for either good or evil.

> For I the LORD thy God am a jealous God, visiting the iniquity of the fathers upon the children unto the third and fourth generation of them that hate me, and showing mercy unto thousands of them that love me and keep my commandments.
>
> —*Deuteronomy 5:9–10*

Personal Reflections:

What causes the negative things that happen around me? Explain how I seek to keep God first in my life.

_____

_____

_____

_____

_____

_____

_____

_____

_____

_____

_____

_____

July 21

If we dare profess Christ yet live contrary to His commandments, we are guilty of sin *(2 John vs. 9–11)*. If we continue to do our own thing, we only deceive ourselves *(Matthew 7:21–23)*. God will not hold us guiltless if we dishonor the price His Son paid at Calvary. We must repent from dead works *(Matthew 15:9)*. Salvation is by grace, and by grace alone *(Ephesians 2:8–10)*.

> Thou shalt not take the name of the LORD thy God in vain: for the LORD will not hold him guiltless that taketh his name in vain.
>
> —*Deuteronomy 5:11*

Personal Reflections:

Have I ever taken the name of the LORD my God in vain? What must I do if I have?

_____

_____

_____

_____

_____

_____

_____

_____

_____

_____

_____

_____

Kathe S. Rumsey & Roberta M. Wong

July 22

Nationally, American culture once honored God's sabbath day. Most businesses remained closed on Sundays; it was a day set apart from the rest of the week. God's plans for mankind's well-being have not changed; He designed the day of rest not for Himself, but for us *(Mark 2:27)*. If we reclaim Sundays for family time and personal relationships, businesses would be impacted and respond accordingly.

> Keep the sabbath day to sanctify it, as the LORD thy God hath commanded thee. Six days thou shalt labor, and do all thy work: but the seventh day is the sabbath of the LORD thy God: in it thou shalt not do any work, thou, nor thy son, nor thy daughter, nor thy manservant, nor thy maidservant, nor thine ox, nor thine ass, nor any of thy cattle, nor thy stranger that is within thy gates; that thy manservant and thy maidservant may rest as well as thou.
>
> *—Deuteronomy 5:12–14*

Personal Reflections:

Explain how the days of the week influence my walk with God. Describe how I choose to spend Sunday that differs from unbelievers.

_____

_____

_____

_____

_____

_____

July 23

Family relationships have suffered tremendously during the past forty years. Children no longer enjoy the secure, nurturing environments that extended families once provided in previous generations. What has the world offered us in exchange for these lost relationships?

Now would be a good time to phone your parents for no reason. Why not renew communications with your grandparents, aunts, uncles, or cousins just for the fun of it. We should be generous with our love to bring back the nurturing environments we once knew. God's heart is all about family and relationships.

> Honor thy father and thy mother, as the LORD thy God
> hath commanded thee; that thy days may be prolonged,
> and that it may go well with thee, in the land which the
> LORD thy God giveth thee.
>
> —*Deuteronomy 5:16*

Personal Reflections:

Have I brought honor to my father and mother even if they did not deserve it? Where has God chosen for me to reside in this world; does it differ from where I have chosen?

_____
_____
_____
_____
_____
_____
_____

July 24

Removal of the Ten Commandments from the walls of America's courtrooms and public buildings does not annul the laws God has written. Spiritually, His laws are still legally binding and reap dire consequences for disobedience *(Galatians 6:7–8)*. In God's eyesight, murder is sin. The penalty for such a crime is determined as each state decides for itself; capital punishment is justified for the crime of murder.

> Thou shalt not kill [murder].
> —*Deuteronomy 5:17*

Personal Reflections:

Explain what the Hebrew word for kill actually means. How does this word clarify the things that take place in our society?

_____

_____

_____

_____

_____

_____

_____

_____

_____

_____

_____

_____

July 25

The Word of God exhorts us to guard our hearts diligently *(Proverbs 4:23)*. When the entertainment industry makes adultery acceptable, we lose our godly perspective of morality. The more we expose ourselves to the world's promotion of ungodly lifestyles and beliefs, the more our sense of biblical discernment will degenerate.

God have mercy on us. Christians must be alert to the seduction of evil, especially when disguised as amusement or virtue. We need to make our choices based on what is acceptable in the sight of God rather than mankind *(Romans 12:1–2)*.

> Neither shalt thou commit adultery.
> *—Deuteronomy 5:18*

Personal Reflections:

Describe how entertainment has influenced the spread of adultery in our world. Explain the consequences of adultery from God's perspective.

Kathe S. Rumsey & Roberta M. Wong

July 26

To consider that Satan entered the heart of Judas Iscariot to betray Jesus for a few pieces of silver should make us wake up. The love of money is the root of all evil *(1 Timothy 6:10)*. To steal anything, no matter how insignificant, is sin; it is a treacherous path to walk. When we think it clever to abuse legitimate business systems for monetary gain, we are guilty of stealing.

Why would we consider it astute to take advantage of those with whom we do business, let alone family, friends, and neighbors? Do not be deceived. With stealing, come serious ramifications *(Romans 8:13)*.

> Neither shalt thou steal.
> —*Deuteronomy 5:19*

Personal Reflections:

Have I taken someone else's property even if it was of no value? Have I accepted too much change from a purchase, and not bothered to return it to the store?

July 27

The Word of God commands us not to speak falsely about others. Additionally, prayer chains do not give us license to meddle in the affairs of others. As God's children, we are not to participate in conversations belittling others, finding fault *(Luke 6:41)*. Our light will not shine brighter by tarnishing the reputation of others. Jesus never criticized others; He came to save lives, not destroy them. When tempted to gossip, we need to learn to bless others, and pray for one another with a sincere heart.

> Neither shalt thou bear false witness against thy neighbor.
> —*Deuteronomy 5:20*

Personal Reflections:

Explain if there was ever a time I could justify speaking evil of a neighbor. What can I do if I slip into a gossip situation with others and discover I am trapped?

_____

_____

_____

_____

_____

_____

_____

_____

_____

_____

July 28

Our life with Christ is not measured by an abundance of material goods *(1 Timothy 6:6)*. Temporary things bring fleeting happiness at best. Hold fast to things of eternal value; the promise of household salvation through Jesus Christ, the Word of God.

> Neither shalt thou desire thy neighbor's wife, neither shalt thou covet thy neighbor's house, his field, or his manservant, or his maidservant, his ox, his ass, or any thing that is thy neighbor's.
>
> —*Deuteronomy 5:21*

Personal Reflections:

Have I ever been envious of something belonging to my neighbor? What should I do when feelings of jealousy attempt to lure me into sin?

_____

_____

_____

_____

_____

_____

_____

_____

_____

_____

_____

_____

_____

July 29

The gods of this age would have us believe the Ten Commandments are expendable and irrelevant. Yet God viewed them indispensable by writing them not only once, but twice *(Exodus 34:1)*. He gave His people the Ten Commandments to protect them from the destruction sin produces. His commandments define and expose sin to warn us away from dangerous paths. We cannot afford to be without these God-given laws in our hearts *(Psalm 119:11)*. Do not be deceived.

> These words the LORD spake unto all your assembly in the mount out of the midst of the fire, of the cloud, and of the thick darkness, with a great voice: and he added no more. And he wrote them in two tables of stone, and delivered them unto me [Moses].
>
> —*Deuteronomy 5:22*

Personal Reflections:

Explain the influence of the Ten Commandments in our culture before they were removed from public buildings. How has the world in which I live changed since they were removed?

_____

_____

_____

_____

_____

_____

_____

_____

Kathe S. Rumsey & Roberta M. Wong

July 30

Just as God gave the nation of Israel instructions to follow when they entered their land of promise, Jesus has given His church commandments to follow Him into our land of promise. In Christ, all God's promises are to us, our children, and our children's children *(Acts 16:31; 2 Corinthians 1:20)*. Do not neglect so great a salvation!

> Now these are the commandments, the statutes, and the judgments, which the LORD your God commanded to teach you, that ye might do them in the land wither ye go to possess it: that thou mightest fear the LORD thy God, to keep all his statutes and his commandments, which I command thee, thou, and thy son, and thy son's son, all the days of thy life; and that thy days may be prolonged.
>
> *—Deuteronomy 6:1–2*

Personal Reflections:

Explain how the church did, or did not, step up to diligently teach the importance of the Ten Commandments after the world removed them. How has God's Word changed concerning its importance in my life?

_____

_____

_____

_____

_____

_____

July 31

What are we teaching our children about the reality of the Living God, the Creator? Tyranny of a few and apathy have allowed the world to remove God and prayer from our public schools. Elimination of the Ten Commandments from public buildings has become the acceptable norm. Our current legislative bodies have redefined evil as good, and good as evil *(Psalm 94:20; Isaiah 5:20)*. God have mercy. Help us to hold back the tidal wave of darkness that attempts to extinguish all light. May we love You with all our heart, soul, strength, mind, and serve only You *(Luke 10:27)*.

> And thou shalt love the LORD thy God with all thine heart, and with all thy soul, and with all thy might. And these words, which I command thee this day, shall be in thine heart: and thou shalt teach them diligently unto thy children, and shalt talk of them when thou sittest in thine house, and when thou walkest by the way, and when thou liest down, and when thou risest up.
>
> *—Deuteronomy 6:5–7*

Personal Reflections:

Explain why I can honestly say I love the LORD my God with all of my being. Have I been faithful in teaching all of God commands to my children, or have I left it up to their Sunday school teacher?

_____

_____

_____

_____

August 1

Unlike the world, God's way is straight and narrow. To achieve victory, it requires courage to resist the flood of compromise that is rampantly sweeping over the earth, and through the church *(James 1:17; 1 John 5:4)*. If we are wise, we will pursue God's will and follow only Him to receive the victor's crown *(James 1:12)*. Remember, we have been purchased with a dear price. Choose this day whom you will serve.

> Only be thou strong and very courageous, that thou mayest observe to do according to all the law, which Moses my servant commanded thee: turn not from it to the right hand or to the left, that thou mayest prosper whithersoever thou goest.
>
> *—Joshua 1:7*

Personal Reflections:

How have I fallen into the deceptive idea that all faiths and churches lead to God? Have I bought into the idea that compromise is okay if it keeps the peace?

_____

_____

_____

_____

_____

_____

_____

_____

August 2

The Word of God, the Bible, is God's operating manual for life. It is inherent in its ability to bring true prosperity and victory. Inspired by God Himself, the Bible reveals within its pages the wisdom and solutions to life's challenges. Spend time and meditate on what the Holy Spirit of God has to say to you concerning your life *(Revelation 2:7)*. Then put His plan into action *(Jeremiah 29:11)*.

> This book of the law shall not depart out of thy mouth; but thou shalt meditate therein day and night, that thou mayest observe to do according to all that is written therein: for then thou shalt make thy way prosperous, and then thou shalt have good success.
>
> *—Joshua 1:8*

Personal Reflections:

What have I faced in this life that has not been addressed in God's Word? If Jesus were to visit my home, where would He find my Bible, Bibles?

_____

_____

_____

_____

_____

_____

_____

_____

_____

_____

August 3

Almighty God is the same yesterday, today and forever. Remember to honor the God of our salvation, Jesus Christ.

> And it shall be, when thou art come in unto the land which the LORD thy God giveth thee for an inheritance, and possessest it, and dwellest therein; that thou shalt take of the first of all the fruit of the earth, which thou shalt bring of thy land that the LORD thy God giveth thee, and shalt put it in a basket, and shalt go unto the place which the LORD thy God shall choose to place his name there.
>
> *—Deuteronomy 26:1–2*

Personal Reflections:

How can I seek God's will in my giving? Explain evidence that suggests God does, or does not, need my resources to get His work done.

_____

_____

_____

_____

_____

_____

_____

_____

_____

_____

August 4

Christian men and women in America should be saddened and outraged at the removal of God's Ten Commandments from public display. Originally written with the finger of God on stone tablets, His commandments were ordained for His people's guidance and protection.

In anger, Moses destroyed the first tablets when he saw God's people dancing and singing, worshipping their man-made idol *(Exodus 32:15–19)*. God's insistence to write His instructions twice demonstrates the importance of these commandments *(Deuteronomy 10:1–2)*.

> And the LORD delivered to me [Moses] two tables of stone written with the finger of God; and on them was written according to all the words, which the LORD spake with you in the mount out of the midst of the fire in the day of the assembly. And it came to pass at the end of forty days and forty nights, that the LORD gave me the two tables of stone, even the tables of the covenant.
>
> *—Deuteronomy 9:10–11*

Personal Reflections:

What is the profound importance of the Ten Commandments? Explain why God replaced the first set that Moses broke if they were as inconsequential as the world would have me believe.

_____

_____

_____

_____

August 5

Sin is sin. With God, there is no compromise. He says what He means, and He means what He says. In due season, obedience to the Word of God will reap blessings only He can bestow. To live like the world and expect to reap God's promises is foolishness.

> Therefore shall ye keep all the commandments which I command you this day, that ye may be strong, and go in and possess the land, whither ye go to possess it; and that ye may prolong your days in the land, which the LORD sware unto your fathers to give unto them and to their seed, a land that floweth with milk and honey.
> —*Deuteronomy 11:8–9*

Personal Reflections:

Describe where God has chosen for me to possess the land. If God placed me in a specific country, should I leave just because I desire a different lifestyle?

_____

_____

_____

_____

_____

_____

_____

_____

_____

August 6

God provided the Ten Commandments not only once, but twice. He did not give them to Moses quietly, as if to conceal them in secret. With the mountain quaking, amidst fire and smoke, His presence commanded full attention. It is foolish to disregard our Creator's Word.

> And he [LORD] wrote on the tables, according to the first writing, the ten commandments, which the LORD spake unto you in the mount out of the midst of the fire in the day of the assembly: and the LORD gave them unto me.
>
> —*Deuteronomy 10:4*

Personal Reflections:

What do the Ten Commandments mean to me? Explain how I base decisions in my life upon these commands.

_____

_____

_____

_____

_____

_____

_____

_____

_____

_____

_____

August 7

Abominations abound as the world becomes increasingly immoral. God's judgment of sin is inevitable. Jesus forewarns of a great tribulation period on the earth *(Matthew 24:21)*. There is an appointed time when an evil world ruler, the son of perdition, will turn in rage against the nation of Israel *(2 Thessalonians 2:3–10)*. When the Holy Spirit and the bride of Christ are taken from the earth, the son of perdition will be completely unrestrained. Pray for Israel. Pray for one another.

> And the king [son of perdition] shall do according to his will; and he shall exalt himself, and magnify himself above every god, and shall speak marvelous things against the God of gods, and shall prosper till the indignation be accomplished: for that that is determined shall be done.
>
> *—Daniel 11:36*

Personal Reflections:

Where have I heard about the son of perdition and his end time role? Explain what God's Word says about spirits of antichrist that are already at work.

_____

_____

_____

_____

_____

_____

August 8

The gospel of *Matthew 25* reveals that just half of those anticipating Christ's arrival will be prepared when He returns for His bride *(1 Thessalonians 4:15–17)*. For the foolish half, the door will shut *(Genesis 7:16)*. Wake up! There is no time to serve the world and God. Make each day count; the great tribulation is for an appointed time.

> And when ye shall see Jerusalem compassed with armies, then know that the desolation thereof is nigh. For these be the days of vengeance, that all things which are written may be fulfilled.
>
> —*Luke 21:20, 22*

Personal Reflections:

What will be my reaction if I see Jerusalem surrounded by her enemies? Describe my understanding of the Bible, and how I can recognize the times in which I live.

August 9

God is longsuffering. It is His will that none should perish *(2 Peter 3:9)*. However, a day is coming when God will judge the whole earth. As devastating as natural disasters have been, they pale in comparison to God's judgment of sin. Does the world approve or disapprove of your principles? If the world rejects you, rejoice *(John 15:18–19)*. Believers of Jesus Christ must continue as light in the midst of darkness until He returns.

> Ah sinful nation, a people laden with iniquity, a seed of evildoers, children that are corrupters: they have forsaken the LORD, they have provoked the Holy One of Israel unto anger, they are gone away backward.
>
> *—Isaiah 1:4*

Personal Reflections:

What evidence suggests my country has come close to crossing the line of no return when it comes to sin? What can I do to help restore her godly foundation?

_____

_____

_____

_____

_____

_____

_____

_____

_____

_____

August 10

How does the immorality of yesterday compare to the current moral collapse? The destruction of Sodom and Gomorrah is for our admonition and example. If we continue in rebellion and refuse God's offer of salvation through grace, we must be willing to accept the consequences of His judgment *(Romans 3:23–25)*. God is a just God. He cannot and will not overlook sin forever.

> Except the LORD of hosts had left unto us a very small remnant, we should have become as Sodom, and we would have been like unto Gomorrah. Come now, and let us reason together, saith the LORD: though your sins be as scarlet, they shall be as white as snow; though they be red like crimson, they shall be as wool. If ye be willing and obedient, ye shall eat the good of the land: but if ye refuse and rebel, ye shall be devoured with the sword: for the mouth of the LORD hath spoken it.
>
> —*Isaiah 1:9, 18–20*

Personal Reflections:

Why is there only a small remnant of committed believers remaining in the world? Why is it important to assemble with other Rock-solid Christians?

_____

_____

_____

_____

_____

_____

Kathe S. Rumsey & Roberta M. Wong

August 11

Every born-again believer has a specific function and place within the body of Christ *(1 Corinthians 12:12)*. We must not delay the work God has called us to complete. A day will come when darkness is so profound that no one will be able to work. Darkness, like an overwhelming flood, erodes even the foundation of neglected tasks for God. What has the Holy Spirit put upon your heart? Begin now, and do not waste a precious moment. Time is running out. Each of us must run the race and complete the work God has asked of us. Redeem this day before the night comes.

> I [Jesus] must work the works of him that sent me, while it is day: the night cometh, when no man can work.
>
> *—John 9:4*

Personal Reflections:

Describe the works God has asked of me that I have put off doing. How will I be able to complete His work as the world becomes darker and darker?

_____

_____

_____

_____

_____

_____

_____

_____

_____

August 12

The invisible, almighty God is known through the written Word of God and revelation by the Holy Spirit. Yet a day will come when the Holy Spirit, the restraining force of evil will be absent *(2 Thessalonians 2:7)*. Time is too precious to waste; the clock is ticking. It is time for the church to wake up and be the light and salt God called her to be. We must love one another more than we thought possible. Pray without ceasing *(1 Thessalonians 5:12–22)*. Our daily choices produce eternal consequences.

> As long as I [Jesus] am in the world, I am the light of the world.
>
> *—John 9:5*

Personal Reflections:

Explain why the world becomes darker and darker as they take God out of our nation. Explain why it is becoming more difficult every year to find a Bible based bookstore, or Bibles in my town, state or nation.

_____

_____

_____

_____

_____

_____

_____

_____

_____

_____

August 13

John the Baptist did not receive a formal education to prepare him for the work God ordained. God planned John's ministry long before his birth, then set it into motion in His perfect time. As members of the body of Christ on earth, God planned a specific purpose and work for us to fulfill.

How is the Holy Spirit preparing you? We are one body but many members *(1 Corinthians 12:12–18)*. Do not be misled by imitating another's role. Follow the Holy Spirit for God's perfect will and time.

> And the child [John] grew, and waxed strong in spirit, and was in the deserts till the day of his showing unto Israel.
>
> *—Luke 1:80*

Personal Reflections:

Describe John's calling on his life and how it makes me desire what God is asking of me. When the enemy attempts to stop me from doing God's will, how can I resist, and not surrender?

_____

_____

_____

_____

_____

_____

_____

_____

August 14

Remarkably, someday the heavens and the earth will pass away, vanish. Unlike the Word of God, they are utterly temporary *(2 Peter 3:10; Revelation 21:1)*. Jesus admonishes His followers to discern the seasons of their lives. What has God asked of you? Do not waste another moment. Watch and pray. Be ready for the Bridegroom's return *(Matthew 25:13)*. We must not disregard the fact that it can occur in our lifetime.

> Now learn a parable of the fig tree; When his branch is yet tender, and putteth forth leaves, ye know that summer is nigh: so likewise ye, when ye shall see all these things, know that it is near, even at the doors. Verily I say unto you, This generation shall not pass, till all these things be fulfilled. Heaven and earth shall pass away, but my words shall not pass away.
>
> *—Matthew 24:32–35*

Personal Reflections:

How can I discern the signs of the times in which I live? What does the significance of Israel becoming a nation in 1948 mean to me?

_____

_____

_____

_____

_____

_____

_____

August 15

Those of the world will not love you; do not be offended by their rejection. Just as the religious rulers of Israel did not receive Jesus Christ, we may be rejected within some congregations when we stand firm on God's Word *(John 1:11)*. Likewise, Apostle Paul did not squander his time disputing with those who rejected truth. He did not try to coax them to believe *(Acts 18:5-6)*.

Do not be troubled or distracted by rejection. Keep moving forward for God. The Son of man, Jesus Christ, comes in an unexpected hour *(Matthew 24:44)*.

> But when they persecute you in this city, flee ye into another: for verily I say unto you, ye shall not have gone over the cities of Israel, till the Son of man be come.
>
> *—Matthew 10:23*

Personal Reflections:

How do I feel when I read that Jesus warned the world would hate me because it hated Him? How should I respond to the hate the world directs toward me?

_____

_____

_____

_____

_____

_____

_____

August 16

The truth of God's Word divides; it is a sword *(Hebrews 4:12–13)*. The world speaks of peace at all costs. That kind of peace will not come no matter who is in authority, no matter what is legislated. Peace between God and mankind came by the Son of God, Jesus Christ. Still the world continues to deny Him. The peace the world seeks is impossible to achieve, but if you accept the price Jesus paid at Calvary for your sins, you can have the Lord's peace in your life *(John 14:27; Colossians 1:20)*.

> Think not that I am come to send peace on earth: I came not to send peace, but a sword.
>
> *—Matthew 10:34*

Personal Reflections:

Rather than be fearful of the division that I observe in my country, do I recognize God's prophetic hand in the breakdown? Would I rather compromise to keep peace, or speak the truth in love?

_____

_____

_____

_____

_____

_____

_____

_____

_____

_____

August 17

True followers of Jesus Christ should never compromise His principles. If our lives radiate the genuine love of Christ, others will see Jesus alive in us. If they receive us, they receive Jesus. If they receive Jesus, they receive God the Father who sent Him. The church does not have to conform to the world to be acceptable to it. Do not be moved or discouraged by their rejection of you or your faith. Put God's love into action and love your enemies; bless, and do not curse them. Pray for those who use and persecute you. Do good to those who hate you. Then you will be like your heavenly Father *(Matthew 5:44–48)*.

> He that receiveth you receiveth me [Jesus], and he that
> receiveth me receiveth him [Father] that sent me.
> *—Matthew 10:40*

Personal Reflections:

Explain how I have felt rejected in my community, or my church. Explain why rejection could lead me towards compromise with the world in order to avoid the pain.

_____

_____

_____

_____

_____

_____

_____

_____

_____

August 18

In *Matthew 24:37–39*, Jesus sets the stage for His return; it is business as usual. Even so, as devoted and grateful as we are to Him, it is possible for the cares, riches, and pleasures of our daily lives to weigh us down. For that reason, the church must be vigilant and continue in prayer. Obedience to God's Word and His Holy Spirit ensures that we will be prepared in His perfect time *(2 Peter 1:5–8)*.

> But as the days of Noah were, so shall also the coming of the Son of man be. For as in the days that were before the flood they were eating and drinking, marrying and giving in marriage, until the day that Noah entered into the ark, and knew not until the flood came, and took them all away; so shall also the coming of the Son of man be.
>
> —*Matthew 24:37–39*

Personal Reflections:

How has God prepared me for the works He has called me to complete? Describe my response when God asks me to do something that seems far from my level of expertise.

_____

_____

_____

_____

_____

_____

_____

August 19

How it must grieve the Holy Spirit of God when He peers into the hearts of mankind! The present-day world exceeds the boundaries of all moral decency, completely without restraint. Congregations cannot point a finger at the world and condemn it when there is just as much perversion in the church. Be admonished; woe to those who corrupt the lives of innocents *(Matthew 18:6)*. God's Spirit will not strive with man forever.

> And the LORD said, My spirit shall not always strive with man, for that he also is flesh: yet his days shall be a hundred and twenty years. And God saw that the wickedness of man was great in the earth, and that every imagination of the thoughts of his heart were only evil continually.
>
> *—Genesis 6:3, 5*

Personal Reflections:

How can I remain focused on ushering in God's light as wickedness increases upon the earth? Describe how my life is pleasing to God according to His Word.

_____

_____

_____

_____

_____

_____

_____

August 20

God knows the end from the beginning. Always faithful to His promises, He provides everything needed in all situations. He will provide a determined defense for the nation of Israel in the end times. Pray for Israel. Pray for the peace of Jerusalem *(Psalm 122:6)*.

> And when the dragon saw that he was cast unto the earth, he persecuted the woman which brought forth the man child. And to the woman were given two wings of a great eagle, that she might fly into the wilderness, into her place, where she is nourished for a time, and times, and half a time, from the face of the serpent. And the serpent cast out of his mouth water as a flood after the woman, that he might cause her to be carried away of the flood.
>
> *—Revelation 12:13–15*

Personal Reflections:

Explain how praying according to God's will assures me that He hears me. What verse gives me faith and hope to believe God has the ability to bring my unsaved loved ones to salvation?

_____

_____

_____

_____

_____

_____

_____

_____

Kathe S. Rumsey & Roberta M. Wong

August 21

A time is coming when Israel's true enemy, the Devil, will be unleashed against her. Only God's divine protection will ensure her survival. So enraged, Satan, the father of all lies, will wage warfare with the remnant of God's people who profess faith in Jesus Christ *(John 8:44; Revelation 12:9)*.

> And the earth helped the woman, and the earth opened her mouth, and swallowed up the flood which the dragon cast out of his mouth. And the dragon was wroth [enraged] with the woman, and went to make war with the remnant of her seed, which keep the commandments of God, and have the testimony of Jesus Christ.
>
> *—Revelation 12:16–17*

Personal Reflections:

Explain the true reason that Israel has so many enemies in this world. Explain why I am committed to follow God's Word and to pray for the peace of Jerusalem.

_____

_____

_____

_____

_____

_____

_____

_____

August 22

Our preparation for our Lord Jesus Christ's return may require obedience of something beyond our experience, just as God required of Noah. Consider the fact no rainfall occurred in his lifetime and yet God commanded Noah to build an ark. Our state of readiness depends upon our obedience of faith *(Matthew 4:4)*.

> And the LORD said unto Noah, Come thou and all thy house into the ark; for thee have I seen righteous before me in this generation. And Noah, went in, and his sons, and his wife, and his sons' wives with him, into the ark, because of the waters of the flood.
>
> *—Genesis 7:1, 7*

Personal Reflections:

How would I feel if Jesus had asked me to come into the ark and to bring my family? Describe what my faith is based upon to believe God's desire is for my entire household to be saved.

_____

_____

_____

_____

_____

_____

_____

_____

_____

_____

Kathe S. Rumsey & Roberta M. Wong

August 23

Absence of God's righteousness paved the way for American society to do what seems right to the individual. People selfishly seek to erect shrines to their personal glory. Greed is unrestrained. How much longer will God allow the pride of mankind to blatantly disregard and dishonor His majesty?

> And the man Micah had a house of gods, and made an ephod, and teraphim, and consecrated one of his sons, who became his priest. In those days there was no king in Israel, but every man did that which was right in his own eyes.
>
> —*Judges 17:5–6*

Personal Reflections:

Describe my own righteousness in contrast to God's righteousness. Describe the things I seek after that are right in my own eyes, but I am not sure about God's perspective.

_____

_____

_____

_____

_____

_____

_____

_____

_____

_____

August 24

How long will we remain foolishly deceived? Sin continues to permeate its dark destruction into every area of our nation. Mankind no longer blushes at perversion, but flaunts it publicly. When will we wake up? *(2 Timothy 3:16–17)*.

> Righteousness exalteth a nation: but sin is a reproach to any people.
>
> —*Proverbs 14:34*

Personal Reflections:

How can I inspire my family and friends to seek after God rather than things and man-made systems? Describe how I have learned to resist the sin that comes from compromising the Bible.

August 25

To compromise truth camouflages sin. The more we concede, the more sin creeps into our lives and takes us captive. Our discernment of sin diminishes when darkness is called light *(Luke 11:34)*. We can no longer foolishly follow the world's ways. In the midst of increasing darkness, while we have opportunity, we must continue to be light. God's Word is our source *(John 1:9)*.

> Arise, shine; for thy light is come, and the glory of the LORD is risen upon thee. For, behold, the darkness shall cover the earth, and gross darkness the people: but the LORD shall arise upon thee, and his glory shall be seen upon thee.
>
> —*Isaiah 60:1–2*

Personal Reflections:

How can I usher in God's light where I see the destructive darkness covering the earth? What allows the Lord's glory to shine upon me as I walk with Him?

_____

_____

_____

_____

_____

_____

_____

_____

_____

August 26

God's covenant with Israel is forever. He is faithful even when mankind is not. Pray for the peace of Jerusalem. Jesus Christ remains the same yesterday, today and forever *(Hebrews 13:8).*

> Lift up your eyes all around, and see: they all gather together, they come to you; your sons shall come from afar, and your daughters shall be nursed at your side, then you shall see and become radiant, and your heart shall swell with joy; because the abundance of the sea shall be turned to you, the wealth of the Gentiles shall come to you. The multitude of camels shall cover your land, the dromedaries of Midian and Ephah; all those from Sheba shall come; they shall bring gold and incense, and they shall proclaim the praises of the LORD.
>
> *—Isaiah 60:4–6 (NKJV)*

Personal Reflections:

Explain why it is important that I make time to pray for the peace of Jerusalem. What country has been committed to the nation of Israel and God's people, and willing to pray for her peace?

_____

_____

_____

_____

_____

_____

_____

Kathe S. Rumsey & Roberta M. Wong

August 27

When we were children, our parents read stories to us. Sometimes at our pleading they would repeat them to satisfy our childish desires. If we are to mature as Christians, we need to understand the principles hidden in Jesus' parables; these reveal the mysteries of the kingdom of God to us. The world's anarchy demands that the church grow up and obey the Word of God. Believers must seek God's will and then do it as the Holy Spirit leads. God is not waiting for the world to do what is right. He is waiting for the church to get right with Him.

> And he [Jesus] said, Unto you it is given to know the mysteries of the kingdom of God: but to others in parables; that seeing they might not see, and hearing they might not understand.
>
> —*Luke 8:10*

Personal Reflections:

Describe how God has made it easy for me to understand His truths. Explain why I am willing to be obedient to His will for my life.

_____

_____

_____

_____

_____

_____

_____

August 28

Get ready. Get ready. Prepare because your future depends upon it. Do not allow yourself to be deceived *(James 1:22)*. The day is coming when the man of sin will deceive the entire world *(2 Thessalonians 2:3–4)*. Each of us is given only one lifetime to get ready for eternity.

> For the mystery of lawlessness is already at work; only He [Spirit of God] who now restrains will do so until He is taken out of the way. And then the lawless one will be revealed whom the Lord will consume with the breath of His mouth and destroy with the brightness of His coming.
>
> *2 Thessalonians 2:7–8 (NKJV)*

Personal Reflections:

How will I be able to recognize the lawless one, the son of perdition when he comes? What if I am still here on earth when he is revealed, what should I do?

_____

_____

_____

_____

_____

_____

_____

_____

_____

Kathe S. Rumsey & Roberta M. Wong

August 29

We, the body of Christ, must purify our lives and walk in truth *(John 17:17, 19; 3 John vs. 4)*. For too many years, we have played church to no avail. Doctrinal and denominational divisions that still exist speak a bewildering gospel to the unsaved world. Jesus prayed that we be one, so that the world may believe in Him *(John 17:21)*. Without sincere, unconditional love, our works misrepresent the kingdom of God to others.

> Seeing ye have purified your souls in obeying the truth through the Spirit unto unfeigned love of the brethren, see that ye love one another with a pure heart fervently: being born again, not of corruptible seed, but of incorruptible, by the word of God, which liveth and abideth forever. But the word [rhema] of the Lord endureth forever. And this is the word [rhema] which by the gospel is preached unto you.
>
> *—1 Peter 1:22–23, 25*

Personal Reflections:

Have I purified my mind, will, and emotions by obeying the truth of the Word of God? Explain what it means for my love to be unconditional.

_____

_____

_____

_____

_____

_____

August 30

Whether times are prosperous or difficult, they are only for a season. God allows us to encounter difficulties that we may overcome the world *(1 John 5:4)*. Just as morning brings activity and night brings rest, there is a purpose for everything under heaven. No matter what the season, God's Word assures us that everything will work for our good *(Romans 8:28)*.

> To every thing there is a season, and a time to every purpose under the heaven.
>
> *—Ecclesiastes 3:1*

Personal Reflections:

Describe the spiritual change of seasons I have witnessed in my lifetime. Why do I place my trust in God to bring me through the storms of life?

_____

_____

_____

_____

_____

_____

_____

_____

_____

_____

_____

_____

August 31

Jesus told us we would receive the Father's promise of the Holy Spirit *(Luke 24:49)*. Group Bible studies are helpful, but they cannot replace private time we spend in God's Word with the Holy Spirit as our teacher. He not only provides us with wisdom, instruction, and direction for our personal lives, but He is the Spirit of truth. The Holy Spirit leads us into all truth *(John 16:17; 1 John 2:27)*.

> But the Comforter, which is the Holy Ghost, whom the Father will send in my name, he shall teach you all things, and bring all things to your remembrance, whatsoever I have said unto you.
>
> *—John 14:26*

Personal Reflections:

Explain how I have submitted to the Holy Spirit as my Comforter and teacher. Explain my desire for Him to lead me according to God's Word.

_____

_____

_____

_____

_____

_____

_____

_____

_____

_____.

September 1

When we wait upon God for guidance, we come to understand that He is the only one who places people and circumstances in our path to make the plans He has for us successful. These encounters may become our biggest challenges. We must trust God in everything at all times. He has our best interest at heart.

> And the man wondering at her held his peace, to wit [know] whether the LORD had made his journey prosperous or not.
>
> —*Genesis 24:21*

Personal Reflections:

How have I learned to trust God to provide for my needs in every circumstance? Explain why I am willing to trust God, even though He may not answer my prayers in my timing.

Kathe S. Rumsey & Roberta M. Wong

September 2

We have a new opportunity in this moment to press on and finish our race here on earth *(2 Timothy 4:7)*. Since the day we accepted Jesus Christ as our Lord and Savior, we continue to be in training. As Christians, we must not become arrogant about our knowledge of eternal life in Jesus Christ *(1 Corinthians 8:1)*. We need to remember it is only by God's grace that we experience eternal life this side heaven.

> Brethren, I count not myself to have apprehended: but this one thing I do, forgetting those things which are behind, and reaching forth unto those things which are before, I press toward the mark for the prize of the high calling of God in Christ Jesus.
> —*Philippians 3:13–14*

Personal Reflections:

Do I hold onto what has been, or look forward to what God is bringing to pass for me? Explain why I trust God with the bad things in my life as well as the good.

September 3

God will supply need but never greed. Our heavenly Father will never provide people and resources that will ultimately harm us or prevent us from attaining His best for our lives *(Romans 8:28)*. He will supply our need according to His plan.

> But my God shall supply all your need according to his riches in glory by Christ Jesus.
>
> *—Philippians 4:19*

Personal Reflections:

When I have asked in faith, has there ever been a genuine need that God has not provided? Explain how I choose to meet other people's needs, or seek the Holy Spirit's leading.

September 4

The never-ending babble of the world attempts to drive us into the pit of despair through its deception. Yet God has provided an escape from the destructive anxiety this clamor produces. Meditate on *Philippians 4:8* rather than the relentless chatter of this world.

> Finally, brethren, whatsoever things are true, whatsoever things are honest, whatsoever things are just, whatsoever things are pure, whatsoever things are lovely, whatsoever things are of good report, if there be any virtue, and if there be any praise, think on these things.
>
> *—Philippians 4:8*

Personal Reflections:

When things test my resolve, do I turn to God's Word to see what is true, honest, just, pure, lovely, and of good report, and if there is virtue, any praise, I think on these? Why do I truly trust God?

_____

_____

_____

_____

_____

_____

_____

_____

_____

September 5

True life and health cannot be found through the things of this world *(Proverbs 18:21)*. A sin-filled world cannot produce life or health. Only God's Word is the true source of life *(John 6:33, 35)*. We must get quiet to hear God's Word, and then apply what we have learned to our life *(3 John vs. 2)*.

> My son, attend to my words; incline thine ear unto my sayings. Let them not depart from thine eyes; keep them in the midst of thine heart. For they are life unto those that find them, and health to all their flesh.
>
> —*Proverbs 4:20–22*

Personal Reflections:

Have I discovered the genuine source of life, and health to all my flesh? Describe why I make the time spent in God's Word a priority.

_____

_____

_____

_____

_____

_____

_____

_____

_____

_____

_____

Kathe S. Rumsey & Roberta M. Wong

September 6

It is vain to look to others for a hopeful life of true and lasting change. Jesus Christ is the Word of God made flesh *(John 1:14)*. Jesus Christ is the bread of life. Jesus Christ is life eternal *(John 17:3; Romans 6:23)*.

> For the bread of God is he which cometh down from heaven, and giveth life unto the world. Verily, verily, I say unto you, He that believeth on me [Jesus] hath everlasting life. I am that bread of life.
>
> *—John 6:33, 47–48*

Personal Reflections:

Explain why I diligently reserve time for God's Word on a daily basis. Describe how I personally know the One who provides everlasting life.

_____

_____

_____

_____

_____

_____

_____

_____

_____

_____

_____

September 7

It is impossible for the Word of God to change. Jesus Christ will never change. He is the same yesterday, today and forever. Even under duress, He would never yield to cultural ethics to please others. He panders to no one. While on earth, Jesus remained focused on the kingdom of God and His Father's righteousness.

As Christians, God's Word mandates our standards; we are to love others unconditionally, without compromising His righteousness.

> So God created man in his own image, in the image of God created he him; male and female created he them. And God blessed them, and God said unto them, Be fruitful, and multiply, and replenish the earth, and subdue it: and have dominion over the fish of the sea, and over the fowl of the air, and over every living thing that moveth upon the earth.
>
> —*Genesis 1:27–28*

Personal Reflections:

How do I know that God created mankind in His image? Explain why I believe He is love and perfection.

_____

_____

_____

_____

_____

_____

Kathe S. Rumsey & Roberta M. Wong

September 8

Because we believe that Jesus Christ is God's Son, our faith will be tried by fire *(1 Peter 1:7; 4:12–13)*. No matter what role we occupy in the body of Christ, we are called to obedience of faith *(Romans 16:25–26)*. We must stand and stand firm to overcome in difficult times. We are called to finish the work God gives us as we diligently prepare ourselves for Christ's return *(Ephesians 2:10; Revelation 19:7)*.

> These words spake Jesus, and lifted up his eyes to heaven, and said, Father, the hour is come; glorify thy Son, that thy Son also may glorify thee: as thou hast given him power over all flesh, that he should give eternal life to as many as thou hast given him. And this is life eternal, that they might know thee the only true God, and Jesus Christ, whom thou hast sent.
>
> *—John 17:1–3*

Personal Reflections:

Explain why I desire eternal life with God Almighty. Explain why I am willing to suffer the consequences of being Jesus' light in the midst of darkness.

_____

_____

_____

_____

_____

_____

_____

September 9

If we continue in Christ and His words continue in us, our heart's motives and desires in everything will be for the glory of God. As our loving Father, God prunes our lives so we can bear more fruit. When our fleshly desires cause us to stray from our Father's will, we must repent. He deserves to be glorified in our lives. It is a daily choice.

> If ye abide in me [Jesus], and my words [rhema] abide in you, ye shall ask what ye will, and it shall be done unto you. Herein is my Father glorified, that ye bear much fruit; so shall ye be my disciples.
>
> —*John 15:7–8*

Personal Reflections:

Describe how I live daily for Christ, allowing His words [rhema] to abide in me. How has my life born fruit in the spiritual realm?

_____

_____

_____

_____

_____

_____

_____

_____

_____

_____

_____

September 10

When we obey God's will in some situations that may appear selfish to our family members, we must take up our cross and exercise patience. It is not always easy to follow Christ. At times, we will be criticized and rejected. When persecutions and challenges come and seem to overwhelm us, we must stand strong and continue to follow Jesus in all things *(2 Corinthians 1:7–11)*. Continue in prayer for your household and trust God *(Acts 16:31)*. He is faithful.

> If any man come to me [Jesus], and hate [love less] not his father, and mother, and wife, and children, and brethren, and sisters, yea, and his own life also, he cannot be my disciple. And whosoever doth not bear his cross, and come after me, cannot be my disciple.
> —*Luke 14:26–27*

Personal Reflections:

Why would I be willing to abandon my family, and my own way of doing things in order to follow Jesus? Explain why my life will be tested as I walk with Christ, and why I will remain committed.

_____

_____

_____

_____

_____

_____

_____

September 11

Luke 13:24 tells us believers will encounter obstacles as we attempt to enter the kingdom of God through the narrow gate *(Acts 14:22)*. For some, these difficult struggles will be more than they are willing to bear. We must press on *(Philippians 3:14)*. Though we do not know when Jesus will return for His bride, we must remain ready *(Revelation 19:7)*.

> Strive to enter in at the strait gate: for many, I say unto you, will seek to enter in, and shall not be able.
>
> *—Luke 13:24*

Personal Reflections:

Explain why being Christian is not easy in many parts of the world. Why I am willing to suffer the pressing as I move through the narrow pathway that leads to eternal life?

_____

_____

_____

_____

_____

_____

_____

_____

_____

_____

_____

Kathe S. Rumsey & Roberta M. Wong

September 12

Once we believe Jesus Christ is the Son of God and has paid the price for our redemption, we must not fritter away the lifetime He has planned for us. To neglect such a gift would be tragic *(Matthew 16:25)*.

> He [Jesus] saith unto them, But whom say ye that I am?
>
> *—Matthew 16:15*

Personal Reflections:

Describe my personal relationship with Jesus Christ. What type of witness for Christ have I been through my lifestyle?

_____

_____

_____

_____

_____

_____

_____

_____

_____

_____

_____

_____

_____

_____

_____

September 13

Let us be grateful, rejoice now and forever that our names are written in heaven. Thank God daily for the priceless gift of eternal salvation that only God Himself could have accomplished. To spend eternity in heaven with Jesus Christ, the King of kings, exceeds the limits of our imagination *(Jude vs. 25)*.

> Behold, I give unto you power to tread on serpents and scorpions, and over all the power of the enemy: and nothing shall by any means hurt you. Notwithstanding in this rejoice not, that the spirits are subject unto you; but rather rejoice, because your names are written in heaven.
>
> *—Luke 10:19–20*

Personal Reflections:

Why do I refuse to give place to the spirit of fear in this world? More importantly, how can I be confident my name is written in Lamb's book in heaven?

_____

_____

_____

_____

_____

_____

_____

_____

_____

September 14

Many a time God will reveal Himself to a new believer because they so easily receive what He offers. They accept the truth with childlike faith. They take Him at His Word. We know God is not influenced by outward appearances, but sees into our heart *(1 Samuel 16:7)*. He will reveal Himself to all whose heart is eager to know Him.

> In that hour Jesus rejoiced in spirit, and said, I thank thee, O Father, Lord of heaven and earth, that thou hast hid these things from the wise and prudent, and hast revealed them unto babes: even so, Father; for so it seemed good in thy sight.
>
> *—Luke 10:21*

Personal Reflections:

Describe what it means to be a baby in the kingdom of God. Describe how I have experienced God's care and leading as a new believer, while receiving the spiritual food I needed to mature.

September 15

No one deserves more praise than the One who has secured our victories. When all appears to crumble around us and we feel alone, rest assured Jesus Christ promises never to forsake us *(Matthew 28:20)*. We can rejoice in Him always no matter what our circumstance may be. He is our Rock. Trust Him *(John 1:14)*.

> Rejoice in the Lord always: and again I say, Rejoice.
> —*Philippians 4:4*

Personal Reflections:

Describe times when I find myself praising him unconsciously. How can I adequately praise God for all He has provided in my life?

_____

_____

_____

_____

_____

_____

_____

_____

_____

_____

_____

_____

_____

Kathe S. Rumsey & Roberta M. Wong

September 16

The enemy's accusations against us before our God have lost all credence and power. They are nothing but empty lies. Jesus' death and resurrection legally grants us the authority and power to overcome the enemy. The blood of the Lamb and our personal testimony attest to the truth of God's salvation. He has provided all we need to obtain victory over the Devil, and the world *(Revelation 12:11)*.

> And I heard a loud voice saying in heaven, Now is come salvation, and strength, and the kingdom of our God, and the power of his Christ: for the accuser [Satan] of our brethren is cast down, which accused them before our God day and night.
>
> *—Revelation 12:10*

Personal Reflections:

Describe my experience of the accuser's burning accusations as the enemy points out my faults. When these torments come, do I stand unwavering upon God's unconditional love and grace?

_____

_____

_____

_____

_____

_____

_____

_____

September 17

This world's problems surge like waves to engulf our mind, will and emotions. Real or imagined, they breed fear. God knows what we need to do and how to accomplish His plan. Jesus had a work to do and so do we *(John 16:33)*. He prayed, "O my Father, if it be possible, let this cup pass from me: nevertheless, not as I will, but as thou wilt" *(Matthew 26:39)*. Listen attentively to the Holy Spirit and walk as He directs.

> And he that overcometh, and keepeth my works unto the end, to him will I give power over the nations: and he shall rule them with a rod of iron; as the vessels of a potter shall they be broken to shivers: even as I received of my Father.
>
> —*Revelation 2:26–27*

Personal Reflections:

What is the Holy Spirit training me to accomplish for God's kingdom? Explain why I am willing to complete the works God created me to accomplish, and in His perfect timing.

_____

_____

_____

_____

_____

_____

_____

_____

_____

Kathe S. Rumsey & Roberta M. Wong

September 18

The Spirit of God still speaks to the body of Christ. The question remains, do we have our ears tuned to His voice? Has the world's clamor distracted and enticed us with its culturally popular babble? Even now, as always, Christ's followers need to be still and wait to hear what God wants to share with us.

> He that hath an ear, let him hear what the Spirit saith unto the churches.
>
> He that hath an ear, let him hear what the Spirit saith unto the churches.
>
> He that hath an ear, let him hear what the Spirit saith unto the churches.
>
> —*Revelation 3:6, 13, 22*

Personal Reflections:

Explain why it is important to have an ear to hear what the Holy Spirit is saying to the churches. What is His message for me, His church, in this season?

_____

_____

_____

_____

_____

_____

_____

_____

_____

September 19

Jesus faced fiery trials as He pressed toward Calvary, His ultimate test of obedience on earth. His victory neither came easily nor without cost. As we follow Christ, we come to appreciate the price He paid as we share in His sufferings. Our fiery trials of faith yield joy unspeakable as we learn more about the One who died for us.

> Beloved, think it not strange concerning the fiery trial which is to try you, as though some strange thing happened unto you: but rejoice, in as much as ye are partakers of Christ's sufferings; that, when his glory shall be revealed, you may be glad also with exceeding joy.
>
> —*1 Peter 4:12–13*

Personal Reflections:

Describe an example where I have been a partaker of Christ's sufferings. Have I experienced fiery trials, yet chose to rejoice because one day His glory shall be revealed?

_____

_____

_____

_____

_____

_____

_____

_____

_____

Kathe S. Rumsey & Roberta M. Wong

September 20

Even though Jesus Christ was sent to serve mankind, He was still all God. He neither demanded the respect nor the attention He rightfully deserved as God; He made Himself of no reputation. For the church to be effective witnesses, we must renew our minds to the truth of Jesus Christ's work and life. He chose to serve rather than to be served. Though innocent, He died among criminals. All glory belongs to the King of kings, the Lord of lords, now and forever. Because of His choice to obey His Father's will, believers inherit eternal life.

> Let this mind be in you, which was also in Christ Jesus: who, being in the form of God, thought it not robbery to be equal with God: but made himself of no reputation, and took upon him the form of a servant, and was made in the likeness of men: and being found in fashion [appearance] as a man, he humbled himself, and became obedient unto death, even the death of the cross.
>
> *—Philippians 2:5–8*

Personal Reflections:

Explain why I am willing to take on the form of a servant instead of a prestigious position within the church. How can I follow Jesus without walking with a servant's heart?

September 21

When spiritual heaviness and the darkness of evil weigh upon us and we feel as though we cannot go on, submitting to the authority of God's Word ensures our protection no matter what we face.

> Submit yourselves therefore to God. Resist the devil,
> and he will flee from you.
>
> —*James 4:7*

Personal Reflections:

How do I submit myself to God? How is it possible for me to resist the enemy?

_____

_____

_____

_____

_____

_____

_____

_____

_____

_____

_____

_____

_____

_____

_____

_____

Kathe S. Rumsey & Roberta M. Wong

September 22

God's mercies are new every morning *(Lamentations 3:22–23).* Do not fear. Do not struggle. Trust your heavenly Father to direct your path and submit to His will with a pure heart. Guard your thoughts from the deceptively twisted influence of this world. Face this moment in time refreshed, knowing God is on your side.

> Draw nigh to God, and he will draw nigh to you. Cleanse your hands, ye sinners; and purify your hearts, ye double minded.
>
> *—James 4:8*

Personal Reflections:

Explain why I desire to reside in God's presence here on earth. How do I utilize the power and authority God has given me for His kingdom?

_____

_____

_____

_____

_____

_____

_____

_____

_____

_____

_____

_____

September 23

In God the Father's perfect time, Jesus Christ will return for His eternal companion, His bride, thus fulfilling God's plan for His Son. Oh, what a day of rejoicing that will be! Remember, the Word of God warns us to be alert and prepared *(Luke 21:34–36)*. Do not be deceived; know that not everyone will be ready *(Matthew 24:36-42; 25:1–13)*.

> Let us be glad and rejoice, and give honor to him: for the marriage of the Lamb is come, and his wife hath made herself ready.
>
> —*Revelation 19:7*

Personal Reflections:

How do I prepare for the return of my Bridegroom, Jesus Christ? Explain what difference it would make to me if I knew my time here on earth was coming to an end.

Kathe S. Rumsey & Roberta M. Wong

September 24

When believers receive revelation of God's Word, a rhema word from the Spirit of God, we will not stumble in the darkness *(Psalm119:130, Matthew 4:4)*. When we finally know God's Word is eternal, we will confidently walk as Jesus walked. We will not walk in fear of what man might do to us.

> His disciples say unto him, Master, the Jews of late sought to stone thee; and goest thou thither [there] again? Jesus answered, Are there not twelve hours in the day? If any man walk in the day, he stumbleth not, because he seeth the light of this world. But if a man walk in the night, he stumbleth, because there is no light in him.
>
> *—John 11:8–10*

Personal Reflections:

Explain why I would walk in boldness if I knew the world hated me and wanted to destroy me. How will I do what needs to be done while there is still light?

_____

_____

_____

_____

_____

_____

_____

_____

September 25

Jesus Christ is the only way to the Father *(John 14:6)*. Hypocrisy and deception abound *(Matthew 7:13–14)*. Seek God with all your heart and He will hear you *(Isaiah 55:3, 6)*. He is not far from each one of us *(Acts 17:24–31)*.

> I have chosen the way of truth: thy judgments have I laid before me.
>
> —*Psalm 119:30*

Personal Reflections:

Explain why I am willing to walk in truth even when it is unpopular. How will I walk in the commandments of God if I have never been taught?

_____

_____

_____

_____

_____

_____

_____

_____

_____

_____

_____

_____

_____

_____

September 26

When God sends us into the world, He provides the necessary light for our safe travel. His Word illuminates our path. The Word of God, true light in us, dispels darkness and enables us to move forward. Our testimony encourages others to live by faith.

> Thy word is a lamp unto my feet, and a light unto my path.
>
> *—Psalm 119:105*

Personal Reflections:

Describe why I will not stumble with His Word to light my way. How does compromise cause my spiritual eyes to adjust to the darkness around me?

_____

_____

_____

_____

_____

_____

_____

_____

_____

_____

_____

_____

_____

September 27

God sent Jesus Christ, the Word made flesh, to redeem all who believe in Him from the curse of the law *(Galatians 3:13)*. God highly exalted His Son and gave Him a name above all names; no other name either in heaven, on earth or under the earth is greater than the name of Jesus *(Philippians 2:9)*. His name greater than the name of every sickness, every condition.

> He sent his word, and healed them, and delivered them from their destructions.
>
> *—Psalm 107:20*

Personal Reflections:

Explain how God's Word is health to all my flesh when I am willing to accept this truth. Explain why God will not give up on me or allow me to be destroyed by the enemy.

_____

_____

_____

_____

_____

_____

_____

_____

_____

_____

_____

_____

_____

September 28

Jesus Christ, the Word made flesh, lived among mankind. He is the Son of God, the Way, the Truth, and the Life *(John 14:16)*. The Word of God is our source of what is real and true in a world inundated with falsehoods and deceptions *(Matthew 24:3–4)*. Glory be to God the Father, God the Son, and God the Holy Spirit! *(1 John 5:7)*.

> And the Word was made flesh, and dwelt among us, (and we beheld his glory, the glory as of the only begotten of the Father,) full of grace and truth.
>
> *—John 1:14*

Personal Reflections:

Explain my personal relationship with Jesus Christ and how it has been life-changing. How much time do I spend in the Word of God on a daily basis?

_____

_____

_____

_____

_____

_____

_____

_____

_____

_____

_____

September 29

If the truth be known, this world has nothing to offer God's children. The world would have us relinquish our birthright in exchange for instant gratification and hollow promises. To know God the Father, God the Son, and God the Holy Spirit in a personal relationship is eternal life here and now.

> And we know that the Son of God is come, and hath given us an understanding, that we may know him that is true, and we are in him that is true, even in his Son Jesus Christ. This is the true God, and eternal life.
>
> —*1 John 5:20*

Personal Reflections:

Have I compromised God's Word, and become accepting of all faiths as truth? Explain why it is not love to know the truth and not share it with others.

_____

_____

_____

_____

_____

_____

_____

_____

_____

_____

_____

_____

Kathe S. Rumsey & Roberta M. Wong

September 30

As we come to know Jesus Christ more intimately, the author and finisher of our faith, it becomes easier to trust in His name *(Hebrews 12:2)*. Through His demonstration of unconditional love at Calvary, Jesus taught us how to live. As we follow His example, we learn to look beyond the faults of others, and even love our enemies *(Ephesians 6:12)*.

> And this is his commandment, That we should believe on the name of his Son Jesus Christ, and love one another, as he gave us commandment.
>
> *—1 John 3:23*

Personal Reflections:

How do I believe that God gave Jesus a name above all names? Describe my love for all of God's children.

_____

_____

_____

_____

_____

_____

_____

_____

_____

_____

_____

_____

October 1

The old saying, *actions speak louder than words,* truly fits this verse. Someone can say repeatedly how much they care for you or that they love you, but their actions speak the loudest. Jesus taught us how to walk in unconditional love for one another. Take time to nurture the relationships with those God has placed in your life.

> My little children, let us not love in word, neither in tongue; but in deed and in truth.
>
> —*1 John 3:18*

Personal Reflections:

What differentiates me, as a child of God, from those who lead a lukewarm Christian life? Explain how I know God's will, and what I should do for others.

_____

_____

_____

_____

_____

_____

_____

_____

_____

_____

_____

_____

Kathe S. Rumsey & Roberta M. Wong

October 2

Because our flesh is weak, there are times when God's children fall into temptation. As difficult as times may be, we must stand guard in faith, and not surrender to circumstances. God's Word instructs us to submit to Him first and then resist the devil *(James 4:7)*. Our Father's faithfulness toward us provides a way of escape for us to endure and encourages us to overcome.

> There hath no temptation taken you but such as is common to man: but God is faithful, who will not suffer you to be tempted above that ye are able; but will with the temptation also make a way to escape, that ye may be able to bear it.
>
> *—1 Corinthians 10:13*

Personal Reflections:

How do I know that the temptations I experience are common to man? Describe how I turn to God in prayer for assistance, and He is faithful to make a way of escape for me.

October 3

Do not be moved by the hate that motivates evil people of this age. When verbal persecution comes for the Word's sake, it is because of God's light in us *(John 3:17–19)*. Those who habitually commit evil hate the light and oppose Jesus Christ. The world hates Jesus. He forewarned that if the world hated Him, it would hate us also.

Stand firm and do not be angered by the words of men, but be encouraged by the Word of God. Our warfare is not against flesh and blood *(Ephesians 6:12)*.

> For every one that doeth [practices] evil hateth the light, neither cometh to the light, lest his deeds should be reproved [exposed].
>
> *—John 3:20*

Personal Reflections:

Explain why the world hates me when I walk in the light of Christ. Why do those of the world avoid those who reflect Jesus' light?

_____

_____

_____

_____

_____

_____

_____

_____

_____

_____

Kathe S. Rumsey & Roberta M. Wong

October 4

When we begin to seek God with all our heart, the Father graciously draws us into everlasting life. To spend eternity anywhere other than in God's presence would be a travesty. God loves the world. He willingly gave His only begotten Son for us so we could know Him as He truly is, and share eternity with Him.

> For God so loved the world, that he gave his only begotten Son, that whosoever believeth in him should not perish, but have everlasting life.
>
> —*John 3:16*

Personal Reflections:

Why should I accept the gift of salvation through grace, rather than count on my works being adequate? Explain why some prefer salvation through works instead of through grace.

_____

_____

_____

_____

_____

_____

_____

_____

_____

_____

_____

_____

October 5

Everyone who competes in a contest wants to receive the crown of victory, but to attain the prize requires sacrifice. God asked an immeasurable sacrifice of Jesus. We must examine our hearts and ask ourselves if we are willing to pay the price God requires of us *(Revelation 12:11)*.

In His wilderness temptations, Jesus resisted and overcame the devil with the Word of God. This same weapon is available to us. When trials come our way, we must endure temptation with faith and patience to receive the crown of life.

> Blessed is the man that endureth temptation: for when
> he is tried, he shall receive the crown of life, which the
> Lord hath promised to them that love him.
>
> —*James 1:12*

Personal Reflections:

Describe how temptations allow my faith to be tested. What must I do to receive the crown of life?

_____

_____

_____

_____

_____

_____

_____

_____

_____

October 6

Each day presents new challenges of faith. Though our path be littered with obstacles, God in His faithfulness promises to rescue us out of harm's way. He makes a way for us that far exceeds anything we could imagine. Rejoice!

> Many are the afflictions of the righteous: but the LORD delivereth him out of them all.
>
> *—Psalm 34:19*

Personal Reflections:

Why will the LORD deliver me out of my harsh conditions? Do I face afflictions because of something I did wrong, or because of something I am doing right for God?

_____

_____

_____

_____

_____

_____

_____

_____

_____

_____

_____

_____

_____

October 7

Our culture requires us to be continuously busy multitasking before others value our efforts. Christians, however, considered foolish and without initiative by those of the world, must exercise patience for God's perfect timing. It is better to be wise in God's eyes. His plans yield a far greater harvest. Wait upon the Lord and renew your strength.

> But they that wait upon the LORD shall renew their strength: they shall mount up with wings as eagles; they shall run, and not be weary; and they shall walk, and not faint.
>
> —*Isaiah 40:31*

Personal Reflections:

Explain why running ahead of God, while attempting to do things in my own strength, will not be successful. What must I learn from this verse about not growing weary in well doing?

_____

_____

_____

_____

_____

_____

_____

_____

_____

_____

October 8

What a glorious thought it is to be a friend of Jesus! When we comprehend the price He paid for us at Calvary, it humbles us. When we grasp the depth of His love and friendship, it motivates us to finish the work He planned for each of us.

> Greater love hath no man than this, that a man lay down his life for his friends. Ye are my friends if ye do whatsoever I command you.
>
> —*John 15:13–14*

Personal Reflections:

Describe my relationship with Jesus Christ: an acquaintance, or my very best friend. What would I call someone who would be willing to lay down their life for mine?

_____

_____

_____

_____

_____

_____

_____

_____

_____

_____

_____

_____

_____

October 9

Our heavenly Father never ceases to love His children. His devotion and commitment are not like ours, weakened by our fickle, feeble natures. Never allow the enemy to deter or distract you with his lies. God, who began His work in us, will continue to renovate and restore our lives. When we stumble, God is not moved; it is only when we give up and stop trying *(Hebrews 10:38)*.

> For I am persuaded, that neither death, nor life, nor angels, nor principalities, nor powers, nor things present, nor things to come, nor height, nor depth, nor any other creature, shall be able to separate us from the love of God, which is in Christ Jesus our Lord.
> —*Romans 8:38–39*

Personal Reflections:

Have I ever truly sensed the love of God in my life, or has He appeared distant? Describe God's promise of drawing near to me if I draw near to Him.

_____

_____

_____

_____

_____

_____

_____

_____

_____

Kathe S. Rumsey & Roberta M. Wong

October 10

With the indoctrination of evolution and the science of genetic research, man has mistakenly convinced himself he is god. Woe to such a notion! Let us sing a new song and rejoice that we know the LORD.

> Make a joyful noise unto the LORD, all ye lands. Serve the LORD with gladness: come before his presence with singing. Know ye that the LORD he is God: it is he that hath made us, and not we ourselves; we are his people, and the sheep of his pasture.
>
> —*Psalm 100:1–3*

Personal Reflections:

How do I view those who believe their purpose on earth is to reconstruct God's creation? Explain why I have so much to rejoice about, beginning with Jesus saving me through grace.

_____

_____

_____

_____

_____

_____

_____

_____

_____

_____

October 11

God may ask us to leave our familiar surroundings, our family, and friends, in order to serve Him. He does not demand these things to make our lives miserable and lonely. Obedience to His commands makes us usable vessels for His purposes *(Luke 9:62)*.

> Now the LORD had said unto Abram, Get thee out of thy country, and from thy kindred, and from thy father's house, unto a land that I will show thee: and I will make of thee a great nation, and I will bless thee, and make thy name great; and thou shalt be a blessing: and I will bless them that bless thee, and curse him that curseth thee: and in thee shall all families of the earth be blessed.
>
> *—Genesis 12:1–3*

Personal Reflections:

Describe how I would feel if God asked me to relocate, leave my relatives, friends, and home. Why would I be willing to give up everything to follow Christ?

_____

_____

_____

_____

_____

_____

_____

_____

Kathe S. Rumsey & Roberta M. Wong

October 12

On Calvary's hill, Jesus became a curse for us *(Galatians 3:13–14)*. Through God's own grace, His undeserved favor, we are ransomed from the "lake of fire. This is the second death" *(Revelation 20:14–15)*. No longer slaves to sin, Jesus Christ is our righteousness before God. We live our lives by faith in Him, and not by works of the law.

> For as many as are of the works of the law are under the curse: for it is written, Cursed is every one that continueth not in all things which are written in the book of the law to do them. But that no man is justified by the law in the sight of God, it is evident: for, The just shall live by faith.
>
> *—Galatians 3:10–11*

Personal Reflections:

How do I encourage my faith to grow? Explain why I am willing to accept God's promises.

October 13

The church must be cautious not to become ensnared in the trap of dead works. God does not require that we earn our own righteousness. It comes only by faith in Jesus Christ and His work of salvation. All who believe in Christ's death and resurrection will inherit eternal life. He alone is our righteousness *(Romans 3:21–25)*.

> For what does the Scripture say? Abraham believed God, and it was accounted to him for righteousness. Now to him who works, the wages are not counted as grace but as debt. But to him who does not work but believes on Him who justifies the ungodly, his faith is accounted for righteousness, just as David also describes the blessedness of the man to whom God imputes righteousness apart from works.
>
> *—Romans 4:3–6 (NKJV)*

Personal Reflections:

How would I describe the benefits of spending time daily with God and His Word? Why is it possible to accept salvation through Jesus Christ by faith, and not by the number of my prayers?

_____

_____

_____

_____

_____

_____

_____

October 14

In total disregard for the Ten Commandments, people live life unrestrained. Selfishness produces havoc and impoverishes many lives. Removal of moral accountability to God within a society, whether it be absent in business, schools, courtrooms or governments, eliminates hope for an orderly, peaceful life.

> Where there is no vision, the people perish: but he that keepeth the law, happy is he.
>
> —*Proverbs 29:18*

Personal Reflections:

Why has the removal of the Ten Commandments created such an impact upon society? Have I even read the Ten Commandments completely, let alone put them into practice?

_____

_____

_____

_____

_____

_____

_____

_____

_____

_____

_____

_____

_____

October 15

God's love and faithfulness are the Rock-solid evidence that endears us to Him. He is our everlasting Rock of tranquility and security. His provisions through His Son Jesus Christ far outweigh in substance and wealth anything the world has to offer. We have a new opportunity to refocus on God and His Word, which allows Him to provide the peace and strength we so desperately seek.

> Thou wilt keep him in perfect peace, whose mind is stayed on thee: because he trusteth in thee. Trust ye in the LORD forever: for in the LORD JEHOVAH is everlasting strength.
>
> *—Isaiah 26:3–4*

Personal Reflections:

Explain what the peace of God means in my life. How do I achieve the peace that is beyond all understanding?

_____

_____

_____

_____

_____

_____

_____

_____

_____

_____

_____

Kathe S. Rumsey & Roberta M. Wong

October 16

God knows our sins. The moment we confess our sin, we can immediately receive forgiveness and be free from its burden. He wants us to confess them for our own health and well-being. This liberty renews our hope and determination to finish the race set before us.

> If we confess our sins, he is faithful and just to forgive
> us our sins, and to cleanse us from all unrighteousness.
> —*1 John 1:9*

Personal Reflections:

Explain why I have falsely held onto my sins foolishly thinking God will overlook them. When I repent of my sin what effect will it have on my relationship with my Lord Jesus?

_____

_____

_____

_____

_____

_____

_____

_____

_____

_____

_____

_____

_____

October 17

Before His departure from earth, Jesus promised His disciples He would send them a Comforter, the Spirit of truth, from the Father *(John 15:26)*. In *1 John 2:27*, Scripture also tells us it is not necessary to rely upon any person to teach us truth because this is the work of the Holy Spirit who abides in us.

Because many false teachers and many false doctrines mislead us into the bondage of dead works, the Spirit of truth that proceeds from the Father is indispensable. The Word of God tells us Jesus fulfilled the law, once, and for all. We must have ears to hear the Holy Spirit and be led of Him. He will guide us into all truth *(John 16:13)*.

> This I say then, Walk in the Spirit, and ye shall not fulfill the lust of the flesh. For the flesh lusteth against the Spirit, and the Spirit against the flesh: and these are contrary the one to the other: so that ye cannot do the things that ye would. But if ye be led by the Spirit, ye are not under the law.
>
> —*Galatians 5:16–18*

Personal Reflections:

Explain what it means to walk in the Spirit. Describe the changes I will make if I am led by God's Spirit.

_____

_____

_____

_____

_____

_____

Kathe S. Rumsey & Roberta M. Wong

October 18

True freedom comes when we die to our own desires and allow the Holy Spirit to direct us in every area of life. As our personal passions are set aside for God's will and kingdom, we gain a real sense of purpose and satisfaction. Even though the life of a Christian may appear blasé to those on the outside, believers know this is far from true. We must not envy the work God is doing in someone else's life. God's children must walk in the gifts He provides. We are all God's workmanship *(Ephesians 2:10)*.

> But the fruit of the Spirit is love, joy, peace, longsuffering, gentleness, goodness, faith, meekness, temperance: against such there is no law. And they that are Christ's have crucified the flesh with the affections and lusts. If we live in the Spirit, let us also walk in the Spirit.
>
> *—Galatians 5:22–25*

Personal Reflections:

Describe the last time I experienced love, joy, and peace in my life. Have I walked in longsuffering, gentleness, goodness, faith, meekness, and temperance, while crucifying my flesh?

_____

_____

_____

_____

_____

_____

October 19

No one comes to the Son of God, Jesus Christ, except God the Father draws him *(John 6:44)*. Jesus chose us and set us apart so that our lives bear fruit, continuously bringing glory to His Father. Whatever we ask in Jesus' name, He will grant it to us. Our heavenly Father will open the doors He has planned for us. Doors that God opens for us no man can shut *(Revelation 3:8)*.

> Ye have not chosen me [Jesus], but I have chosen you, and ordained you, that ye should go and bring forth fruit, and that your fruit should remain: that whatsoever ye shall ask of the Father in my name, he may give it you. These things I command you, that ye love one another.
>
> *—John 15:16–17*

Personal Reflections:

How can I fully comprehend the fact that Jesus chose me? Explain why Jesus' love towards me makes it possible for me to love others.

_____

_____

_____

_____

_____

_____

_____

_____

October 20

The world's misinformation would have us pulled in one direction and then, another. Even news reports, as misconstrued as they may be, serve as a reminder that our opportunity is limited. It is time to submit to what God would have us do and guard ourselves from worldly distractions.

Ephesians 5:15–17 warns us to redeem our time because we live in evil days. Faith is too precious a gift to waste. There is coming a time when no man can work *(John 9:4–5)*. We need to be wise and redeem the time God has allotted us.

> And he said, Take heed that ye be not be deceived: for many shall come in my name, saying, I am Christ; and the time draweth near: go ye not therefore after them. But when ye shall hear of wars and commotions, be not terrified: for these things must first come to pass; but the end is not by and by.
>
> *—Luke 21:8–9*

Personal Reflections:

Although identifying as Christian, some churches have become businesses; will I be able to differentiate which ones are truly His? How am I able to discern the seasons and times of the end?

_____

_____

_____

_____

_____

_____

October 21

Most Christians presume they will be Christ's bride upon His return. Wake up! Only believers who have oil in their vessels will be ready when Jesus arrives *(Matthew 25:11–13)*. Pressure upon mature fruit yields the oil *(John 15:1–16)*. Do not run from the tests and trials of your faith. Seek God with all your heart *(James 1:2–4)*.

> And the foolish said unto the wise, Give us of your oil; for our lamps are gone out. But the wise answered, saying, Not so; lest there be not enough for us and you: but go ye rather to them that sell, and buy for yourselves. And while they went to buy, the bridegroom came; and they that were ready went in with him to the marriage: and the door was shut.
>
> —*Matthew 25:8–10*

Personal Reflections:

As Christ's return gets closer, will I be among the foolish who have not prepared, or among the wise? Once the door is shut, if I am left because of my foolishness, will the door open again?

_____

_____

_____

_____

_____

_____

_____

_____

_____

Kathe S. Rumsey & Roberta M. Wong

October 22

Soldiers do not enter battle by targeting their fellow soldiers. They train by diligent preparation, consistently following orders from their commander-in-chief.

Likewise, as Christians, other people are not the root cause of our discontent and agitation. Our battle is not against flesh and blood. We are called to be soldiers in God's army. Prepare for spiritual battle; put on the whole armor of God, and then stand, and stand firm.

> Put on the whole armor of God, that ye may be able to stand against the wiles of the devil. For we wrestle not against flesh and blood, but against principalities, against powers, against the rulers of the darkness of this world [age], against spiritual wickedness in high places. Wherefore take unto you the whole armor of God, that ye may be able to withstand in the evil day, and having done all, to stand.
>
> —*Ephesians 6:11–13*

Personal Reflections:

What is the motivation behind the evil behaviors of our day? Explain what I must do to put on the full armor of God in order to stand when the enemy comes against me.

October 23

Only Jesus makes it possible for us to overcome the trials and temptations of this world. Belief in the only begotten Son of God, who died and then rose again, is the key to overcoming the world. Spend time with Jesus, the Word of God *(John 1:1)*.

> For this is the love of God, that we keep his commandments: and his commandments are not grievous. For whatsoever is born of God overcometh the world: and this is the victory that has overcometh the world, even our faith. Who is he that overcometh the world, but he that believeth that Jesus is the Son of God?
>
> —*1 John 5:3–5*

Personal Reflections:

Explain why it is possible for me to overcome this world. Where does my faith to overcome originate?

_____

_____

_____

_____

_____

_____

_____

_____

_____

_____

_____

October 24

Each member of the body of Christ has a specific function to fulfill. We know that God is no respecter of persons; He values each one of us equally. Because we are a body interdependent upon one another, it is necessary to be in one accord if we hope to complete God's work on earth. Believers must operate within their rightful position in the body of Christ. It is time for the church to get into God's order with Christ as head in everything.

> For I say, through the grace given unto me, to every man that is among you, not to think of himself more highly than he ought to think; but to think soberly, according as God hath dealt to every man the measure of faith. For as we have many members in one body, and all members have not the same office [function]: so we, being many, are one body in Christ, and every one members one of another.
>
> —*Romans 12:3–5*

Personal Reflections:

Why would we think more highly of ourselves than a brother since it was Jesus Christ who purchased salvation for each of us? Explain why I cannot increase my faith in my own strength.

_____

_____

_____

_____

_____

_____

October 25

Faith is a gift from God. It comes by hearing the Holy Spirit as He reveals the Word of God to us. As we act upon what we hear and apply what we know to be true, we will experience victory in our lives. Faith overcomes the world.

> So then faith cometh by hearing, and hearing by the word [rhema] of God.
>
> —*Romans 10:17*

Personal Reflections:

What is the Holy Spirit saying to the churches? Describe a situation where I have heard a rhema word for a specific situation from God through His Spirit.

_____

_____

_____

_____

_____

_____

_____

_____

_____

_____

_____

_____

_____

_____

October 26

Even the most nutritious meal is still insufficient to our well-being in comparison to each Word God reveals to us through Scripture. His Words [rhema] are "spirit and they are life" *(John 6:63)*. When was the last time you enjoyed a satisfying meal in God's Word? The Bible provides health and balance for our spiritual immune system.

> But he [Jesus] answered and said, It is written, Man shall not live by bread alone, but by every word [rhema] that proceedeth out of the mouth of God.
>
> *—Matthew 4:4*

Personal Reflections:

Describe a time when I asked my Pastor if he had received a rhema word from God, and if so, how could I? Will the Holy Spirit freely move in my church congregation, or be limited by a fixed agenda?

October 27

Throughout the world, this Scripture continues to be relevant. Christians must pray; for when there are few laborers, a harvest can be lost.

> Then saith he [Jesus] unto his disciples, The harvest truly is plenteous, but the laborers are few; pray ye therefore the Lord of the harvest, that he will send forth laborers into his harvest.
>
> —*Matthew 9:37–38*

Personal Reflections:

What should be my plan of action when I read the harvest is ready? Explain why I pray for God to send laborers into His fields.

Kathe S. Rumsey & Roberta M. Wong

October 28

As we listen to the nightly news, we can discern the signs of the times and Jesus' eminent return. When the Father tells His Son it is time, Christ will come for His bride *(1 Thessalonians 4:16)*. *Daniel 7:25* tells us in the last days a king will arise, an evil ruler, that will speak pompously against God. This wicked ruler will persecute God's people and be given power to change laws and times. Many antichrists are already at work, preparing the way for the man of sin, the son of perdition *(2 Thessalonians 2:3–8; 1 John 2:18)*.

> Behold, I will send my messenger, and he shall prepare the way before me: and the Lord, whom ye seek, shall suddenly come to his temple, even the messenger of the covenant, whom ye delight in: behold, he shall come, saith the LORD of hosts.
>
> *—Malachi 3:1*

Personal Reflections:

What can I do to be wise and ready for Christ's return if it should take place during my lifetime? Describe situations where mankind is already attempting to change times and laws.

_____

_____

_____

_____

_____

_____

October 29

An intimate relationship with the Holy Spirit of God will change your life. He is the Spirit of truth, our Comforter and teacher, our daily prayer partner. If you have not asked your heavenly Father for this priceless gift, now is a great opportunity *(Luke 24:49)*.

> If ye then, being evil, know how to give good gifts unto your children: how much more shall your heavenly Father give the Holy Spirit to them that ask him?
>
> *—Luke 11:13*

Personal Reflections:

Explain why I should ask God for the baptism with the Holy Spirit. Describe the moment when I trusted Him to provide me with my prayer language *(Ephesians 6:18)*.

_____

_____

_____

_____

_____

_____

_____

_____

_____

_____

_____

_____

_____

Kathe S. Rumsey & Roberta M. Wong

October 30

God's Word shows us true charity comes from the heart without outward displays. The world is quite the opposite. Many high schools in America currently require mandatory community service before graduation. It is not voluntary, yet touted as such. Because it is difficult to discern someone's true need, we must seek the Holy Spirit as to what He would have us do. Then, quietly obey without public demonstration.

> Take heed that you do not do your charitable deeds
> before men, to be seen by them. Otherwise you have
> no reward from your Father in heaven. Therefore,
> when you do a charitable deed, do not sound a trumpet
> before you as the hypocrites do in the synagogues and
> in the streets, that they may have the glory from men.
> Assuredly, I say to you, they have their reward.
>
> —*Matthew 6:1–2 (NKJV)*

Personal Reflections:

Explain how I seek wisdom from the Holy Spirit as to what charitable deeds I should participate in and how often. What motivates me to give to an organization, or to give in my workplace?

_____

_____

_____

_____

_____

_____

October 31

Halloween has become a business enterprise of enormous proportions. As Christians, why do we feel compelled to provide an alternative and call it a harvest festival so our children will not feel left out? Dressing up as biblical characters and handing out candy changes nothing. When our churches offer activities as alternatives to Halloween, we must ask ourselves how this brings honor to God. Is it pleasing to Him? We are to live differently from the world, not imitate it *(Deuteronomy 12:28–32; Luke 16:15; John 8:12; 17:14–19; Romans 12:1–2; 2 Corinthians 6:15–18; 1 John 2:15–17).*

> And this is the condemnation, that light is come into the world, and men loved darkness rather than light, because their deeds were evil. For every one that doeth evil hateth the light, neither cometh to the light, lest his deeds should be reproved. But he that doeth truth cometh to the light, that his deeds may be made manifest, that they are wrought in God.
>
> *—John 3:19–21*

Personal Reflections:

Why would I camouflage evil deeds? Explain why others might avoid me when they sense the presence of Christ Jesus residing in me.

Kathe S. Rumsey & Roberta M. Wong

November 1

We live in perilous times *(2 Timothy 3:1-9)*. As children of God looking to the world's systems for solutions, we are left crippled by its ideologies and opinions. Our lives should be established upon God's kingdom principles. Our unresolved problems are rooted in our failure to surrender our will to God and seek His wisdom and direction for our lives. With God, all things are possible.

> Therefore, I say unto you, Take no thought for your
> life, what ye shall eat, or what ye shall drink; nor yet
> for your body, what ye shall put on. Is not the life more
> than meat, and the body than raiment?
> —*Matthew 6:25*

Personal Reflections:

What is God's plan and purpose for my life here on earth? How do the cares of this world keep me from focusing on my walk with Christ Jesus?

_____

_____

_____

_____

_____

_____

_____

_____

_____

_____

November 2

Our heavenly Father has promised to provide for all our needs *(Philippians 4:19)*. As members of His family, God's children are not dependent upon men's institutions.

> But seek ye first the kingdom of God, and his righteousness; and all these things shall be added unto you.
>
> *—Matthew 6:33*

Personal Reflections:

Should I look to government, or to God to meet my needs? If I lack essentials of life, where can I go to have my needs met?

_____

_____

_____

_____

_____

_____

_____

_____

_____

_____

_____

_____

_____

_____

Kathe S. Rumsey & Roberta M. Wong

November 3

In rebellion against God and His Word, our culture calls good evil, and evil good *(Isaiah 5:20)*. From every direction, corruption seduces individuals to accept the mores of a degenerate world.

Christians are not to blindly follow the dictates of men. When evil parades as good, mankind has lost its God-given ability to discern right from wrong. Stand for righteousness, and stand firm.

> It is not good to show partiality to the wicked, or to overthrow the righteous in judgment.
> —*Proverbs 18:5 (NKJV)*

Personal Reflections:

Describe how the world shows favoritism to the wicked, while rejecting Christians. Explain how laws are being changed to provide loopholes for the criminal element in our society.

_____

_____

_____

_____

_____

_____

_____

_____

_____

_____

_____

_____

_____

November 4

Daily, believers have an opportunity to serve God or this world in everything we do. We must humble ourselves and pray *(Proverbs 18:12)*. It is only by the grace of God that it is possible for us to communicate with Him and know His will.

> Be not deceived; God is not mocked: for whatsoever a man soweth, that shall he also reap. For he that soweth to his flesh, shall of the flesh reap corruption; but he that soweth to the Spirit shall of the Spirit reap life everlasting.
>
> *—Galatians 6:7–8*

Personal Reflections:

Explain why sowing hate and discord will not produce a harvest of love and unity. When I pander to my flesh and put my relationship with God on hold, will I experience a victorious life?

_____

_____

_____

_____

_____

_____

_____

_____

_____

_____

_____

November 5

Scripture defines faith as substance of things hoped for, evidence of things we do not see *(Hebrews 11:1)*. When obstacles prevent us from moving forward in the kingdom of God, words of faith can remove them. In the name of Jesus, we can speak to them and they must obey *(Philippians 2:9–11)*. The gates of hell cannot prevail against the church.

> And the Lord said, If ye had faith as a grain of mustard seed, ye might say unto this sycamine tree, Be thou plucked up by the root, and be thou planted in the sea; and it should obey you.
>
> *—Luke 17:6*

Personal Reflections:

How much faith do I need to move the destructive obstacles in my life? Explain what it means to have mustard seed size faith.

_____

_____

_____

_____

_____

_____

_____

_____

_____

_____

_____

November 6

God is faithful. Our ability to accomplish something may not seem realistic, but with God all things are possible. Believe. Do not doubt in your heart. You will have what you say.

> Have faith in God. For verily I say unto you, That whosoever shall say unto this mountain, Be thou removed, and be thou cast into the sea; and shall not doubt in his heart, but shall believe that those things which he saith shall come to pass; he shall have whatsoever he saith.
>
> —*Mark 11:22–23*

Personal Reflections:

How do I utilize the authority Jesus has given me in His name? Explain how the victories in my life are possible, because of what I do, or because of God.

_____

_____

_____

_____

_____

_____

_____

_____

_____

_____

_____

Kathe S. Rumsey & Roberta M. Wong

November 7

Godly wisdom is first pure, without selfish motives. Then it is amiable, calm, compassionate, forgiving and noble. It is without duplicity. In contrast, worldly wisdom is arrogant, divisive, harsh, biased. God has made His wisdom available to those who ask Him. The wise believer will seek God's pure and unselfish wisdom in all matters.

> But the wisdom that is from above is first pure, then peaceable, gentle, willing to yield, full of mercy and good fruits, without partiality and without hypocrisy. Now the fruit of righteousness is sown in peace by those who make peace.
> —*James 3:17–18 (NKJV)*

Personal Reflections:

What kind of knowledge do I seek: godly wisdom, or worldly wisdom? Explain why I have been known in my family as the peacemaker.

_____

_____

_____

_____

_____

_____

_____

_____

_____

November 8

False doctrine spreads like leaven throughout the Christian community, affecting everyone and everything it touches. Unless we know the truth, we will not be able to recognize the counterfeit. Pray and seek God's face to know His genuine, unleavened Word.

> Then Jesus said to them [His disciples], Take heed and beware of the leaven of the Pharisees and the Sadducees. Then they understood that He did not tell them to beware of the leaven of bread, but of the doctrine of the Pharisees and Sadducees.
>
> —*Matthew 16:6, 12 (NKJV)*

Personal Reflections:

When I listen to someone preach either at church or at a Christian conference, am I able to discern if it is biblically based, or a worldly trend? Explain why words of compromise are like leaven.

_____

_____

_____

_____

_____

_____

_____

_____

_____

_____

_____

Kathe S. Rumsey & Roberta M. Wong

November 9

When you find yourself in a competitive work environment, remember to guard your heart. Do not allow envy and selfish ambition to rule. If others around you are causing contention, know that confusion and evil will be present. Do not return evil for evil.

> But if ye have bitter envying and strife in your hearts, glory not, and lie not against the truth. This wisdom descendeth not from above, but is earthly, sensual, devilish. For where envying and strife is, there is confusion and every evil work.
>
> —*James 3:14–16*

Personal Reflections:

Explain why I would not want to allow envy and strife to take hold of my heart, and influence everything I do. When I find myself in the midst of confusion, how do I quickly discern the evil work taking place?

November 10

We can encourage others to grow and develop their strengths. When we observe someone doing something well, we can let them know how much we appreciate their effort. As a nation, we have reinforced bad behavior far too long, while ignoring the good. It is time to reinforce the good in others. Genuine love edifies.

> Let each of you look out not only for his own interests,
> but also for the interests of others.
> —*Philippians 2:4 (NKJV)*

Personal Reflections:

When I am with others do I look out for their best interest? Describe how I have been selfish lately, looking out only for my comfort and ease, and how it made me feel later.

_____

_____

_____

_____

_____

_____

_____

_____

_____

_____

_____

_____

_____

November 11

Patience only comes by standing firm on God's Word when our faith is tested. When we actively resist sin's temptations and obey God's commandments, we will develop the patience of Jesus. As we take up our cross daily and follow Him, we become true disciples of our Lord Jesus Christ *(Matthew 16:24–25; Luke 14:27)*.

> My brethren, count it all joy when ye fall into divers temptations; knowing this, that the trying of your faith worketh patience. But let patience have her perfect work, that ye may be perfect and entire, wanting nothing.
>
> *—James 1:2–4*

Personal Reflections:

Explain why temptations will not destroy me, and how I should consider it all joy when I am confronted by one. How has my patience increased while I take up my cross daily?

_____

_____

_____

_____

_____

_____

_____

_____

_____

_____

_____

November 12

The church can walk confidently, knowing Jesus is the author and finisher of our faith *(Hebrews 12:2)*. When we realize God's continued faithfulness to transform us into the person He created us to be, we can rejoice. Equally devoted to finishing the work He began in all His children, we can run the race He has set before us.

> I thank my God upon every remembrance of you, always in every prayer of mine for you all making request with joy, for your fellowship in the gospel from the first day until now; being confident of this very thing, that he which hath begun a good work in you will perform it until the day of Jesus Christ.
>
> *—Philippians 1:3–6*

Personal Reflections:

How often do I thank God for the wonderful believers He has placed in my life? Describe how He who began a good work in me will use the changes in me to make a difference in the world.

_____

_____

_____

_____

_____

_____

_____

_____

_____

_____

Kathe S. Rumsey & Roberta M. Wong

November 13

God has a plan for each of us *(2 Timothy 1:9)*. When the enemy attempts to distract or discourage us, we must look to the Word of God and the Holy Spirit to get us through our daily conflicts *(Philippians 4:3)*.

> Wherefore seeing we also are compassed about with so great a cloud of witnesses, let us lay aside every weight, and the sin which doth so easily beset us, and let us run with patience the race that is set before us, looking unto Jesus, the author and finisher of our faith; who for the joy that was set before him endured the cross, despising the shame, and is set down at the right hand of the throne of God.
>
> *—Hebrews 12:1–2*

Personal Reflections:

Describe how I have identified the weights and the sin that holds me back from being all God desires for me to be. Explain why I am confident I will finish the race set before me.

_____

_____

_____

_____

_____

_____

_____

_____

November 14

When we abandon our own willful ways and acknowledge God in all our decisions, He will guide us along the path He has planned for us. He knows precisely what He created each one of us to accomplish. He has our future mapped out for us. Precious time is wasted when we try to figure out our future. To have more intimacy with the evil ways of the world than to know God in a personal relationship is an abomination by any standard *(Jeremiah 4:22; Luke 16:15; James 4:4)*.

> Trust in the LORD with all thine heart; and lean not unto thine own understanding. In all thy ways acknowledge him, and he shall direct thy paths.
>
> *—Proverbs 3:5–6*

Personal Reflections:

Explain God's plan for my life, and how I faithfully walk in it. Who, if anyone, is more deserving of my faith and trust than Christ Jesus?

_____

_____

_____

_____

_____

_____

_____

_____

_____

Kathe S. Rumsey & Roberta M. Wong

November 15

Wives are to love and respect their own husbands. God will do the rest.

> Likewise, ye wives, be in subjection to your own husbands; that, if any obey not the word, they also may without the word be won by the conversation [conduct] of their wives; while they behold your chaste conversation coupled with fear [respect].
>
> —*1 Peter 3:1–2*

Personal Reflections:

If my husband does not follow God's Word, but I submit to him, will he be won over by my conduct? If my husband is wrong, but I defer to him, will God intervene in the situation?

_____

_____

_____

_____

_____

_____

_____

_____

_____

_____

_____

_____

_____

_____

November 16

The marketing media of this world would have our daughters believe that what they wear and how they look is what makes them beautiful and have value. Young women are so devastated by these standards that they fail to develop the inner, incorruptible attributes of a gentle and quiet spirit. As a community of believers, we must help the young women in our congregations to see themselves as God's beloved daughters. They are daughters of the King of kings. They are members of the royal family of God.

> Do not let your beauty be that outward adorning of arranging the hair, of wearing gold, or of putting on fine apparel; but let it be the hidden person of the heart, with the incorruptible ornament of a gentle and quiet spirit, which is very precious in the sight of God.
> —*1 Peter 3:3–4 (NKJV)*

Personal Reflections:

Why do I spend more time and energy on my outward appearance than on my inner being? Is Jesus looking for me to have outward beauty as His bride, or inner beauty and character?

_____

_____

_____

_____

_____

_____

_____

_____

November 17

As we grow in Christ, our lives will encounter seasons of trials. The Holy Spirit reminds us to hear His voice. We must not harden our hearts toward God when times are tough, but let our lives shine for Him. How we respond in these fiery trials is a greater witness of our faith in God. Our actions speak louder than words to an unsaved world.

> Wherefore (as the Holy Ghost saith, Today if ye will hear his voice, harden not your hearts, as in the provocation, in the day of temptation in the wilderness: when your fathers tempted me, proved me, and saw my works forty years. Wherefore I was grieved with that generation, and said, They do always err in their heart; and they have not known my ways. So I swore in my wrath, They shall not enter my rest.)
>
> —*Hebrews 3:7–11*

Personal Reflections:

Would I rather know God's ways, or do things my own way? Describe a situation where I have witnessed someone who has hardened their heart toward God, and how I responded toward them.

_____

_____

_____

_____

_____

_____

November 18

The world glorifies rebels but God's Word calls rebellion witchcraft. As God's children, we have His authority to intercede for righteousness to prevail *(Psalm 125:3)*. Through humility and prayer, God promises to heal our land *(2 Chronicles 7:14)*.

To outlaw God and remove His standard of righteousness from every aspect of life is to find ourselves living in the midst of witchcraft and idolatry. It is the church's responsibility to pray to establish God's will and kingdom on earth.

> For rebellion is as the sin of witchcraft, and stubbornness is as iniquity and idolatry.
>
> *—1 Samuel 15:23*

Personal Reflections:

Explain how I can prevent a rebellious spirit from manipulating me. How do I avoid becoming a slave to idolatry?

_____

_____

_____

_____

_____

_____

_____

_____

_____

_____

_____

_____

Kathe S. Rumsey & Roberta M. Wong

November 19

Do you know the reputation of your community, your state? Do Christians freely acknowledge their faith in Jesus Christ and honor God? No matter where we reside as Christians, we must keep ourselves blameless before our God.

> When you come into the land which the LORD your God is giving you, you shall not learn to follow the abominations of those nations. There shall not be found among you anyone who makes his son or his daughter pass through the fire, or one who practices witchcraft, or a soothsayer, or one who interprets omens, or a sorcerer, or one who conjures spells, or a medium, or a spiritist, or one who calls up the dead. For all who do these things are an abomination to the LORD, and because of these abominations the LORD your God drives them out from before you. You shall be blameless before the LORD your God.
>
> —*Deuteronomy 18:9–13 (NKJV)*

Personal Reflections:

How can I avoid following the abominations of the land in which the LORD my God is giving me? If I am involved in witchcraft (rebellion) or anything involving a medium, how can I be set free?

_____

_____

_____

_____

_____

November 20

For any society to dismiss God and reject His commandments, and then substitute acceptance of evil spirits and witchcraft is to invite sheer destruction *(1 Timothy 4:1–4)*. God created mankind to worship Him alone. Wake up! To accept the notion that there is no God will eventually bring its own judgment.

> I will cut off sorceries from your hand, and you shall have no soothsayers. Your carved images I will also cut off, and your sacred pillars from your midst; you shall no more worship the work of your hands; I will pluck your wooden images from your midst; thus I will destroy your cities. And I will execute vengeance in anger and fury on the nations that have not heard.
> —*Micah 5:12–15 (NKJV)*

Personal Reflections:

When society rejects God, gives place to soothsayers, sorceries, and worship the artwork they create, how will I find safety in their cities? What if I participate in events inspired by wizardry?

_____

_____

_____

_____

_____

_____

_____

_____

_____

Kathe S. Rumsey & Roberta M. Wong

November 21

In *Mark 1:15*, the word *time* refers to opportune time, due season, due time. The kingdom of God is available right now for anyone who has a change of heart and believes the good news of Jesus Christ. Repent and believe.

> The time is fulfilled, and the kingdom of God is at
> hand: repent ye, and believe the gospel.
>
> —*Mark 1:15*

Personal Reflections:

Explain how I have learned to trust God's Word in every area of my life. How do I witness to the victory that Christ Jesus has provided for me?

_____

_____

_____

_____

_____

_____

_____

_____

_____

_____

_____

_____

_____

_____

November 22

Amid material abundance, many genuine needs in our society, neighborhoods and church families remain unnoticed and unfulfilled. As a nation, we cannot expect government services to meet every need. Pray and ask God where He would have you meet a need for Him.

> As we have therefore opportunity, let us do good unto
> all men, especially unto them who are of the household
> of faith.
>
> —*Galatians 6:10*

Personal Reflections:

If I want to walk in truth, how am I to treat others, especially other believers? Describe how I have learned to seek wisdom from the Holy Spirit as to what contributions will be a blessing to others.

_____

_____

_____

_____

_____

_____

_____

_____

_____

_____

_____

_____

Kathe S. Rumsey & Roberta M. Wong

November 23

God's enemies are our enemies. When we are weak, God is strong and faithful *(2 Corinthians 12:9)*. Submit to His Word, resist the devil and our adversary will flee *(James 4:7)*. Be strong in the Lord. Put on the whole armor of God before you leave home *(Ephesians 6:10–18)*.

> Finally, my brethren, be strong in the Lord, and in the power of his might. Put on the whole armor of God, that ye may be able to stand against the wiles of the devil. For we wrestle not against flesh and blood, but against principalities, against powers, against the rulers of the darkness of this world [age], against spiritual wickedness in high places.
>
> *—Ephesians 6:10–12*

Personal Reflections:

How do I suit up in the whole armor of God when challenges come? People are not my enemies; how do I recognize what spirit is manipulating these individuals?

_____

_____

_____

_____

_____

_____

_____

_____

November 24

To spend our lifetime on earth without a personal relationship with Jesus Christ, and then to have Him reject us for all eternity is an overwhelming thought *(Matthew 7:21–23)*. We must die daily to selfishness, so that we may live in Him. Stand, and stand firm when faced with trials. Now is not the time to give up and quit. Jesus promised not to forsake us or leave us even to the end of the age *(Matthew 28:20)*.

> Therefore I endure all things for the elect's sakes, that they may also obtain the salvation which is in Christ Jesus with eternal glory. It is a faithful saying: For if we be dead with him, we shall also live with him: if we suffer, we shall also reign with him: if we deny him, he also will deny us: if we believe not, yet he abideth faithful: he cannot deny himself.
>
> *—2 Timothy 2:10–13*

Personal Reflections:

How would I feel if Jesus denied knowing me? Is it possible to pick and choose what I am willing to endure in this life?

_____

_____

_____

_____

_____

_____

_____

Kathe S. Rumsey & Roberta M. Wong

November 25

For those who have a personal relationship with the Holy Spirit of God, to blaspheme Him is unthinkable.

> Wherefore I [Jesus] say unto you, All manner of sin and blasphemy shall be forgiven unto men: but the blasphemy against the Holy Ghost shall not be forgiven unto men. And whosoever speaketh a word against the Son of man, it shall be forgiven him: but whosoever speaketh against the Holy Ghost, it shall not be forgiven him, neither in this world [age], neither in the world to come.
>
> —*Matthew 12:31–32*

Personal Reflections:

How does it make me feel when I hear someone rejecting the Holy Spirit's role on earth? Since Jesus has paid for everything on my behalf, how do I receive the baptism with the Holy Spirit?

_____

_____

_____

_____

_____

_____

_____

_____

_____

_____

November 26

God's Word is alive and full of hope. His love never fails. In our unfaithfulness, He remains faithful. He never abandons His people. His mercy endures forever. Pray for one another. Pray for Israel.

> Behold, the days come, saith the LORD, that the plowman shall overtake the reaper, and the treader of grapes him that soweth seed; and the mountains shall drop sweet wine, and all the hills shall melt. And I will bring again the captivity of my people of Israel, and they shall build the waste cities, and inhabit them; and they shall plant vineyards, and drink the wine thereof; they shall also make gardens, and eat the fruit of them.
>
> —*Amos 9:13–14*

Personal Reflections:

When I hear someone speaking evil of Israel, how should I react? What would God like for me to do on behalf of Israel?

_____

_____

_____

_____

_____

_____

_____

_____

_____

_____

Kathe S. Rumsey & Roberta M. Wong

November 27

It is high time to be debt free. Our heavenly Father knows our need of earthly things but Jesus reminds us of our priorities (Matthew 6:33). It is God's desire that His children owe no one anything but love *(Romans 13:8)*.

> Woe to him who increases what is not his—how long? And to him who loads himself with many pledges? Will not your creditors rise up suddenly? Will they not awaken who oppress you? And you will become their booty.
>
> *—Habakkuk 2:6–7 (NKJV)*

Personal Reflections:

Explain why shopping binges, and running up debt are not wise. Would I choose to be hounded by debtors because of something that has no heavenly value?

_____

_____

_____

_____

_____

_____

_____

_____

_____

_____

_____

November 28

God's Word speaks to His people, not to the world. His warnings are for us. Wake up, church. We will reap what we sow.

> Woe to you who plunder, though you have not been plundered; and you who deal treacherously, though they have not dealt treacherously with you! When you cease plundering, you will be plundered; and when you make an end of dealing treacherously, they will deal treacherously with you.
>
> —*Isaiah 33:1 (NKJV)*

Personal Reflections:

Explain how I should deal with someone who attempts to utterly destroy me. As a child of God, how do I deal with someone who betrays me?

_____

_____

_____

_____

_____

_____

_____

_____

_____

_____

_____

_____

November 29

After Jesus returned to His Father in heaven, born-again believers became God's family representatives on earth. We are ambassadors for His kingdom, endowed with Christ's authority *(Luke 10:19)*. We can choose to embody God's graciousness and unconditional love, or we can be like rebellious children demanding our own way. Let us choose to be salt and light in a world that is perishing *(Matthew 5:13–16)*.

> Therefore, being justified by faith, we have peace with God through our Lord Jesus Christ: by whom also we have access by faith into this grace wherein we stand, and rejoice in hope of the glory of God. And not only so, but we glory in tribulations also: knowing that tribulation worketh patience; and patience, experience; and experience, hope: and hope maketh not ashamed; because the love of God is shed abroad in our hearts by the Holy Ghost which is given unto us.
>
> *—Romans 5:1–5*

Personal Reflections:

Describe how tribulation in my life brings patience, experience, hope, and why I must not reject the challenges as a part of my training. Is the Holy Spirit available to believers in this generation?

Right-side-up in an Upside-down World   333

November 30

The world's best offer cannot compare to the righteousness of Jesus Christ and His companionship for all of eternity.

> For a day in thy courts is better than a thousand. I had rather be a doorkeeper in the house of my God, than to dwell in the tents of wickedness. O LORD of hosts, blessed is the man that trusteth in thee.
>
> —*Psalm 84:10, 12*

Personal Reflections:

Explain why I would prefer to be a servant in the house of my God, and not be an elitist in the power realm of this world. How do I put my full trust in God Almighty?

_____

_____

_____

_____

_____

_____

_____

_____

_____

_____

_____

_____

_____

_____

_____

December 1

Faith in Jesus Christ is the only way to eternal life. We cannot do anything to earn it. Eternal life is a free gift, undeserved and unmerited.

> For by grace are ye saved through faith; and that not
> of yourselves: it is the gift of God: not of works, lest
> any man should boast.
>
> —*Ephesians 2:8–9*

Personal Reflections:

Explain how I can honestly accept salvation through grace, and not by my works in the church. How will I be able to repay Jesus for the door He opened for me that leads to eternal life?

_____

_____

_____

_____

_____

_____

_____

_____

_____

_____

_____

_____

_____

December 2

Our lives need to reflect the peace of God in the midst of a troubled world. We have the opportunity to triumph over tribulation by the grace of God. When we finally know that His Word is eternal, we will confidently walk as Jesus walked. We do not need to be anxious regarding anything or anyone. Let the peace of God guard your mind and heart, knowing Jesus has overcome the world *(John 16:33; Philippians 4:5, 7).*

> Be not thou therefore ashamed of the testimony of our Lord, nor of me [Paul] his prisoner: but be thou partaker of the afflictions of the gospel according to the power of God; who hath saved us, and called us with a holy calling, not according to our works, but according to his own purpose and grace, which was given us in Christ Jesus before the world began, but is now made manifest by the appearing of our Savior Jesus Christ, who hath abolished death, and hath brought life and immortality to light through the gospel.
>
> *—2 Timothy 1:8–10*

Personal Reflections:

What must I do to obtain eternal life? God called me, but my works profit me nothing, why?

_____

_____

_____

_____

_____

Kathe S. Rumsey & Roberta M. Wong

December 3

In turbulent times, God alone stabilizes our soul *(1 Peter 5:10)*. His wisdom is available to us in all circumstances. Our confidence needs to rest in His faithfulness. Jesus is our Rock.

> Now to him [God] that is of power to establish you according to my gospel, and the preaching of Jesus Christ, according to the revelation of the mystery, which was kept secret since the world began, but now is made manifest, and by the Scriptures of the prophets, according to the commandment of the everlasting God, made known to all nations for the obedience of faith: to God only wise, be glory through Jesus Christ forever. Amen.
>
> *—Romans 16:25–27*

Personal Reflections:

Since Jesus Christ is the only One who could redeem me from eternal separation, what can I offer to do for Him? How should I live after Jesus paid such a great price for my redemption?

_____

_____

_____

_____

_____

_____

_____

_____

December 4

Politicians, financial consultants, university professors, medical professionals operate on limited knowledge. Modern day think tanks try their best to solve problems, but usually produce more chaos. As we face an uncertain future reliant upon the world's systems, we can turn to God's Word and the guidance of the Holy Spirit for true wisdom to ensure our livelihood. Jesus Christ alone is all-knowing. We do not need to fear. God controls all. His throne is eternal *(Psalm 11:1–7)*.

> To the only wise God our Savior, be glory and majesty, dominion and power, both now and ever. Amen.
>
> *—Jude vs. 25*

Personal Reflections:

Explain why all glory and majesty belong to Jesus Christ. How do I use the power Jesus has given me?

_____

_____

_____

_____

_____

_____

_____

_____

_____

_____

_____

December 5

Walk liberated in the good news of Jesus Christ. God the Father accepted His Son's payment for our sin debt; we have passed from death into life *(Colossians 1:19–20).* By faith, we are holy, blameless and without reproach in God's sight. Continue to grow in the precious gift of grace and faith.

> And you, that were sometime alienated and enemies in your mind by wicked works, ye now hath he reconciled in the body of his flesh through death, to present you holy and unblamable and unreprovable in his sight: if ye continue in the faith grounded and settled, and be not moved away from the hope of the gospel, which ye have heard, and which was preached to every creature which is under heaven; whereof I Paul am made a minister.
> —*Colossians 1:21–23*

Personal Reflections:

How can my relationship with God be restored since wicked works alienate me from Him? What does it mean to be debt free in the spiritual realm?

_____

_____

_____

_____

_____

_____

_____

December 6

Principalities and powers, the spiritual forces of this age, wage war against the body of Jesus Christ on earth. The church should not be intimidated; the gates of hell cannot prevail against her *(Matthew 16:18–19; Ephesians 6:10–18)*. Put on the whole armor of God to overcome all the obstacles the enemy uses to obstruct our way. Rejoice. The name of Jesus is greater than all. He is with us wherever we go.

> They shall fight against thee; but they shall not prevail against thee; for I am with thee, saith the LORD, to deliver thee.
>
> *—Jeremiah 1:19*

Personal Reflections:

Explain why I have nothing to fear with Jesus' promise to deliver me from the hand of the enemy. How do I utilize the full armor of God?

_____

_____

_____

_____

_____

_____

_____

_____

_____

_____

Kathe S. Rumsey & Roberta M. Wong

December 7

Mankind blindly surrounds itself with idols as a means of comfort and fulfillment. When we realize that true and lasting satisfaction comes from a personal relationship with our Creator and heavenly Father, then idols lose their attraction. God created us in His image. Jesus Christ remains the same yesterday, today and forever *(Hebrews 13:8)*. Nothing and no one can replace the emptiness we experience apart from knowing God.

> Thus saith the LORD, What iniquity have your fathers found in me, that they have gone far from me, and have walked after vanity [idols] and are become vain?
>
> —*Jeremiah 2:5*

Personal Reflections:

Explain why it is important to avoid making the same mistakes my father made before me. Why does my heavenly Father desire a personal relationship with me?

_____

_____

_____

_____

_____

_____

_____

_____

_____

_____

December 8

It is absurd foolishness to expect God to bless America when our nation recklessly forsakes Him for other gods. We have exchanged God's glory for dumb idols, thinking we can solve our problems. Mankind is a fragile vessel. Apart from God, we can do nothing. He alone is our source; no system of governance can ever replace Him. Before it is too late, America must restore honor to God whom our forefathers acknowledged as worthy.

> Hath a nation changed their gods, which are yet no gods? but my people have changed their glory for that which doth not profit. Be astonished, O ye heavens, at this, and be horribly afraid, be ye very desolate, saith the LORD. For my people have committed two evils; they have forsaken me the fountain of living waters, and hewed them out cisterns, broken cisterns, that can hold no water.
>
> *—Jeremiah 2:11–13*

Personal Reflections:

When have I been indifferent to the removal of God from the public arena? Why does God remove His protection when a nation's people have hardened their hearts, and where does that leave me?

_____

_____

_____

_____

_____

_____

December 9

Now is a good time to take inventory of what needs to change in our life, and then we must set these changes into motion. If we forsake God and succumb to the darkness of this age, we put our future in jeopardy *(Hebrews 12:5–11)*.

> Thine own wickedness shall correct thee, and thy backslidings shall reprove thee: know therefore and see that it is an evil thing and bitter, that thou hast forsaken the LORD thy God, and that my fear is not in thee, saith the Lord GOD of hosts.
>
> *—Jeremiah 2:19*

Personal Reflections:

How does compromise in the church effect Bible believing Christians? Explain why Christians can no longer say the world is evil, without admitting the same thing is taking place in churches.

_____
_____
_____
_____
_____
_____
_____
_____
_____
_____
_____

December 10

God's love never fails. He has not abandoned us. On the other hand, mankind has forsaken Him. Some have feverishly attempted to erase the truth of God's existence, hoping to eliminate accountability and responsibility. To think we can replace God's wisdom with our own standard of righteousness is a deceptive and foolish notion.

> If thou wilt return, O Israel, saith the LORD, return unto me: and if thou wilt put away thine abominations out of my sight, then shalt thou not remove. And thou shalt swear, The LORD liveth, in truth, in judgment, and in righteousness; and the nations shall bless themselves in him, and in him shall they glory.
>
> *—Jeremiah 4:1–2*

Personal Reflections:

What abominations have been secretly hidden under the cloak of righteousness within the church? What can I do as a believer to rid the church of these deceptive practices?

_____

_____

_____

_____

_____

_____

_____

_____

_____

Kathe S. Rumsey & Roberta M. Wong

December 11

What a powerful difference the Word of God would make if husbands and wives valued His wisdom! A society stubbornly refusing God's principles foolishly undermines the strength of marriage and solid family values.

> Therefore as the church is subject unto Christ, so let the wives be to their own husbands in every thing. Husbands, love your wives, even as Christ also loved the church, and gave himself for it; that he might sanctify and cleanse it with the washing of water by the word [rhema], that he might present it to himself a glorious church, not having spot, or wrinkle, or any such thing; but that it should be holy and without blemish.
>
> —*Ephesians 5:24–27*

Personal Reflections:

What would Christ throw out of the church first if He were on earth at this time in history? Explain why I need a rhema word from God Almighty if I desire to see the temple washed and sanctified.

_____

_____

_____

_____

_____

_____

_____

December 12

No matter what happens in the world around us, we must stand firm in faith. Stand, and do not depart from the hope promised in the gospel of Jesus Christ, our Lord and Savior *(Colossians 1:19–20).*

> And you, that were sometime alienated and enemies in your mind by wicked works, yet now hath he [Jesus] reconciled...if ye continue in the faith grounded and settled, and be not moved away from the hope of the gospel, which ye have heard, and which was preached to every creature which is under heaven; where of I Paul am made a minister.
>
> *—Colossians 1:21, 23*

Personal Reflections:

How will Jesus treat our relationship if I seek forgiveness from Him through repentance? Explain how I have found a solid Bible-believing church to attend.

_____

_____

_____

_____

_____

_____

_____

_____

_____

_____

Kathe S. Rumsey & Roberta M. Wong

December 13

If we are the children of God, we are in the world, not of the world. We must be wise and understand what it means to speak with a perverse mouth. This refers to a person who speaks a corrupt message. To speak of immoral things as respectable, and honorable things as evil, is extreme wickedness. It is crucial as we walk in this life that we neither imitate nor conform to the world's ways *(Romans 12:1–2).*

> A worthless person, a wicked man, walks with a perverse mouth; he winks with his eyes, he shuffles his feet, he points with his fingers; perversity is in his heart, he devises evil continually, he sows discord.
> *—Proverbs 6:12–14 (NKJV)*

Personal Reflections:

How can I justify a close relationship with the world, and claim to be a Christian? Why does wickedness rule the world in greater degrees than in years past?

_____

_____

_____

_____

_____

_____

_____

_____

_____

_____

December 14

In due season, Jesus will return suddenly, without warning. Those who behave unjustly will continue to do so. Likewise, those who pursue holiness will remain on the path they chose. As members of the body of Christ, each one of us has a work to finish. It is our responsibility to know what our heavenly Father wants us to accomplish in our allotted season.

> Seal not the sayings of the prophesy of this book: for the time is at hand. He that is unjust, let him be unjust still: and he which is filthy, let him be filthy still: and he that is righteous, let him be righteous still: and he that is holy, let him be holy still. And, behold, I [Jesus] come quickly; and my reward is with me, to give every man according as his work shall be.
>
> —*Revelation 22:10–12*

Personal Reflections:

Have I personally studied the Book of Revelation? Describe why the study of this book is of great benefit to me.

_____

_____

_____

_____

_____

_____

_____

_____

_____

Kathe S. Rumsey & Roberta M. Wong

December 15

Sometimes when we read in Jude, "mockers in the last time," we falsely assume it is a confirmation of the final moments of history *(Jude vs. 18–19)*. However, this passage shows us that impostors have infiltrated among true believers since the church age began at Pentecost *(Acts 2:1–4)*. Therefore, we must continue to walk in the truth of the gospel, increasing in faith and love *(Colossians 1:3–6)*. Christians should live in such a way that others may desire God's blessings of forgiveness in their lives.

> But ye, beloved, building up yourselves on your most
> holy faith, praying in the Holy Ghost, keep yourselves
> in the love of God, looking for the mercy of our Lord
> Jesus Christ unto eternal life.
>
> *—Jude vs. 20–21*

Personal Reflections:

What does it mean to pray in the Holy Spirit? Describe Scripture references that prove whether the Holy Spirit was, or was not, accessible only at the beginning of the church age.

_____

_____

_____

_____

_____

_____

_____

_____

December 16

The body of Christ must pray, help one another, and not rely upon government handouts to meet our needs. As God's children diligently seek Him through His Word, He will prepare us for our future and any challenges we may face. He is more than able to supply our daily provisions. God designed His work plan long ago, knowing how to benefit mankind *(Exodus 20:8–11)*. In His kingdom, there is no lack.

> Go to the ant, thou sluggard; consider her ways, and be wise: which having no guide, overseer, or ruler, provideth her meat in the summer, and gathereth her food in the harvest.
>
> *—Proverbs 6:6–8*

Personal Reflections:

Describe how I have been wise in my walk with Jesus Christ. What am I willing to invest to deepen my relationship with Christ?

_____

_____

_____

_____

_____

_____

_____

_____

_____

_____

_____

Kathe S. Rumsey & Roberta M. Wong

December 17

The Book of James tells us faith without works is dead. Wake up. Wake up! The hour is late, yet not too late to begin anew. Time is precious. We must not permit the powers of darkness to seduce us into slumber nor distract us from our Father's will. Now is the most opportune time to accomplish God's work in history.

> How long wilt thou sleep, O sluggard? when wilt thou arise out of thy sleep? Yet a little sleep, a little slumber, a little folding of the hands to sleep: so shall thy poverty come as one that traveleth, and thy want as an armed man.
>
> *—Proverbs 6:9–11*

Personal Reflections:

What has happened in our nation as the church partied with the world? Explain what to say to believers concerning the programs of the world that are used to entice people into church pews.

_____

_____

_____

_____

_____

_____

_____

_____

_____

_____

December 18

God truly has our best interest at heart. He gently encourages us to live by faith and trust Him. If our love is genuine, we will keep His commandments and obey Him *(John 14:15).*

> For the commandment is a lamp; and the law is light; and reproofs of instruction are the way of life: to keep thee from the evil woman, from the flattery of the tongue of a strange woman [seductress].
>
> *—Proverbs 6:23–24*

Personal Reflections:

What inspires me to walk in God's plan for my life? Describe how His commandments are for my protection.

_____

_____

_____

_____

_____

_____

_____

_____

_____

_____

_____

_____

_____

_____

December 19

God does not need the assistance of modern day think tanks to help Him resolve the problems of this world. His wisdom exceeds the so-called knowledge of the world. What God desires of His people are humility, prayer and obedience. Let's humble ourselves before Him and He will heal our world *(2 Chronicles 7:14)*. Apply the wisdom of God that you find in His Word to guide you in all things.

> I wisdom dwell with prudence, and find out knowledge
> of witty inventions. Counsel is mine, and sound
> wisdom: I am understanding: I have strength. By me
> kings reign, and princes decree justice. By me princes
> rule, and nobles, even all the judges of the earth.
> —*Proverbs 8:12, 14–16*

Personal Reflections:

How will I be successful in this life without God's wisdom? Describe how I might seek God's wisdom and apply it to the needs of my country.

_____

_____

_____

_____

_____

_____

_____

_____

_____

December 20

The body of Christ eagerly awaits the day when we can thank Jesus Christ face to face.

> To God our Savior, Who alone is wise, be glory and majesty, dominion and power, both now and forever. Amen.
>
> —*Jude vs. 25 (NKJV)*

Personal Reflections:

Explain my personal relationship with God, my Savior. How am I to operate in Jesus' authority and power here on earth?

_____

_____

_____

_____

_____

_____

_____

_____

_____

_____

_____

_____

_____

_____

_____

_____

December 21

Harvest season is ever present. Each day in which God gives us breath is a day to gather the harvest. Even though windows of opportunity seem limited, pray and ask the Lord of the harvest to send forth laborers into His harvest *(Matthew 9:37–38)*. It is not too late.

> He that gathereth in summer is a wise son: but he that sleepeth in harvest is a son that causeth shame.
> —*Proverbs 10:5*

Personal Reflections:

What is the perfect time for the harvest of souls? How have I prayed for God to send laborers into His fields?

_____

_____

_____

_____

_____

_____

_____

_____

_____

_____

_____

_____

_____

_____

_____

December 22

Out of the abundance of a wicked heart proceeds babble, lies, and confusion. Out of the abundance of a righteous heart comes health and life. As Christians, we must choose our words carefully. God's Holy Spirit in us provides words of inspiration to share with believers and unbelievers.

> In the multitude of words sin is not lacking, but he who restrains his lips is wise. The tongue of the righteous is choice silver; the heart of the wicked is worth little.
> —*Proverbs 10:19–20 (NKJV)*

Personal Reflections:

Will I be able to distinguish a child of God from a child of the devil by their words? Explain why I appreciate the words of a righteous one in contrast to one that spews vile and destructive words.

Kathe S. Rumsey & Roberta M. Wong

December 23

As Christians, do we seek God's standard of good with due diligence? Have dead works entrapped us, while presumptuously thinking God is pleased with our service to Him? *(Matthew 7:21–23)*. If our goal is to serve God to fulfill His will only, we will find His favor. He rewards those who diligently seek Him *(Hebrews 11:6)*.

> He that diligently seeketh good procureth favor.
> —*Proverbs 11:27*

Personal Reflections:

How has the presence of God become a priority in my life? Explain why I live to know His wisdom, and to sit at His feet.

_____

_____

_____

_____

_____

_____

_____

_____

_____

_____

_____

_____

_____

_____

December 24

God's children can trust their heavenly Father to meet their needs even in the midst of a collapse of this world's systems. In Christ, we can calmly face the future with assurance, knowing nothing takes God by surprise. His wisdom is available to us in all circumstances. God has promised to meet all our need; we can trust His Word *(Philippians 4:19)*.

> A good man leaveth an inheritance to his children's children: and the wealth of the sinner is laid up for the just.
>
> —*Proverbs13:22*

Personal Reflections:

Explain how I count on God to pass the inheritance of a praying family member down to my children and grandchildren. Why am I confident God's provision will pass down to my household?

_____

_____

_____

_____

_____

_____

_____

_____

_____

_____

_____

Kathe S. Rumsey & Roberta M. Wong

December 25

The greatest gift given to the whole world is God's gift of our Lord and Savior Jesus Christ! To celebrate December 25th and salute others with Happy Holidays does not alter the significance this day represents. Jesus Christ's life, death and resurrection are the only reasons to celebrate a Merry Christmas. Take away Jesus and you eliminate the reason for celebrating.

> For God so loved the world, that he gave his only begotten Son, that whosoever believeth in him should not perish, but have everlasting life.
>
> —*John 3:16*

Personal Reflections:

What is my view of everlasting life? Why did God send Jesus to be sacrificed for the sins of the whole world?

_____

_____

_____

_____

_____

_____

_____

_____

_____

_____

_____

_____

_____

December 26

To speak the truth in love brings edification and comfort to the hearer. Do not allow the intimidation of others to prevent you from speaking the truth. Jesus never told people what they wanted to hear. He told them what they needed to hear. Hypocrisy of any kind misleads and keeps people in bondage.

> He that speaketh truth showeth forth righteousness: but a false witness deceit. There is that speaketh like the piercings of a sword: but the tongue of the wise is health.
>
> —*Proverbs 12:17–18*

Personal Reflections:

What is different about the words that come from a wise believer? Describe how I seek God's wisdom daily, so that I may be part of the solution rather than the problem.

_____

_____

_____

_____

_____

_____

_____

_____

_____

_____

_____

December 27

Rejoice! The King of kings, the Lord of lords is with us. Jesus Christ has overcome the world. He has conquered death and hell. Jesus promises never to leave us nor forsake us even to the end of the age *(Matthew 28:20).*

> Oh, clap your hands, all you peoples! Shout to God
> with the voice of triumph! For the LORD Most High
> is awesome; He is a great King over all the earth.
> He will subdue the peoples under us, and the nations
> under our feet.
>
> *—Psalms 47:1–3 (NKJV)*

Personal Reflections:

How do I demonstrate my adoration for all the LORD Most High has done on my behalf? Describe how it would sound if I shout and sing of His love and power all day, all week, all month, all year.

_____

_____

_____

_____

_____

_____

_____

_____

_____

_____

_____

December 28

God has showered His mercy upon us through Jesus Christ, His Son *(Revelation 1:5)*. We must not take God's generous gift for granted, neglecting so great a salvation.

> Have mercy upon me, O God, according to thy lovingkindness: according unto the multitude of thy tender mercies blot out my transgressions. Wash me throughly from mine iniquity, and cleanse me from my sin.
>
> —*Psalms 51:1–2*

Personal Reflections:

Describe God's salvation that washed away my sins and forgave my iniquity. Explain how I desire to be in His presence all day long.

_____

_____

_____

_____

_____

_____

_____

_____

_____

_____

_____

_____

_____

December 29

God placed in the heart of every person a desire to worship Him. Even remote cultures around the world, free from outside influence, seek to worship their gods. That alone should be evidence to the fool that God exists *(Psalm 19:1–6)*.

> The fool hath said in his heart, There is no God.
> Corrupt are they, and have done abominable iniquity:
> there is none that doeth good.
>
> *—Psalms 53:1*

Personal Reflections:

What is it going to be like in eternity for the fool that claims there is no God? Have I been such a fool at one time or another during my lifetime?

_____

_____

_____

_____

_____

_____

_____

_____

_____

_____

_____

_____

December 30

Help us Father to run our race and be victorious overcomers. May we walk worthy of our Lord Jesus Christ, our first love *(Revelation 2:4).*

> God looked down from heaven upon the children of men, to see if there were any that did understand, that did seek God. Every one of them is gone back: they are altogether become filthy; there is none that doeth good, no, not one.
>
> *—Psalms 53:2–3*

Personal Reflections:

What does God observe me doing when He looks down at me? Describe changes I can make in my life that will please my heavenly Father and my Lord Jesus Christ, rather than please the world.

_____

_____

_____

_____

_____

_____

_____

_____

_____

_____

_____

_____

Kathe S. Rumsey & Roberta M. Wong

December 31

Only by God's grace and mercy, we stand before tomorrow to accomplish His work on this side of eternity.

> Save me, O God, by thy name, and judge me by thy strength. Hear my prayer, O God; give ear to the words of my mouth. Behold, God is mine helper: the Lord is with them that uphold my soul. He shall reward evil unto mine enemies: cut them off in thy truth.
>
> —*Psalm 54:1–2, 4–5*

Personal Reflections:

What does God do when I cry out because my enemies are overwhelming me? How does He respond to the evil acts of my enemies?

_____

_____

_____

_____

_____

_____

_____

_____

_____

_____

_____

_____

_____

_____

About the Authors

In 1983, Kathe Rumsey's life was radically turned right-side-up following a series of relatively insignificant events: a class reunion, a neighborhood craft group that evolved into a Bible study. Through her determination to discover genuine purpose in life, she came to know Jesus Christ as her Lord and Savior. Kathe grew up in a Christian home and traditional denomination. Later, receiving the gift of the baptism with the Holy Spirit, Kathe has undeniably experienced God's faithfulness. The Word of God is her Rock-solid basis for all her life choices. She resides in Washington State with her husband and family.

Born again in 1985, Roberta Wong received Jesus Christ into her heart and was baptized with God's Holy Spirit. She experienced God's powerful intervention and life eternal began. Rescued from the darkness of false doctrines, the Bible became her source of light! The Spirit of truth became her teacher and the kingdom of God unfolded before her. Roberta came to know the Father, the Son and the Holy Spirit. As she delved into the Word of God, she discovered that Jesus Christ is truly the Bread of life. She and her husband reside in Washington State.

Kathe S. Rumsey and Roberta M. Wong have also coauthored or authored:
~ *Love Is the Commitment: Protocol Guidelines for God's Royal Wedding*; ~ *The Lamb's Wife Makes Herself Ready: Love Is the Commitment Bible Study Workbook with Commentary*; ~ *Tell that Bully, No! The Overcomer's Handbook*.